We Will Trust

Even When it Hurts

KELLY R. HENLEY

WESTBOW
PRESS®
A DIVISION OF THOMAS NELSON
& ZONDERVAN

Copyright © 2020 Kelly R. Henley.

All rights reserved. No part of this book may be used or reproduced by any means, graphic, electronic, or mechanical, including photocopying, recording, taping or by any information storage retrieval system without the written permission of the author except in the case of brief quotations embodied in critical articles and reviews.

WestBow Press books may be ordered through booksellers or by contacting:

WestBow Press
A Division of Thomas Nelson & Zondervan
1663 Liberty Drive
Bloomington, IN 47403
www.westbowpress.com
844-714-3454

Because of the dynamic nature of the Internet, any web addresses or links contained in this book may have changed since publication and may no longer be valid. The views expressed in this work are solely those of the author and do not necessarily reflect the views of the publisher, and the publisher hereby disclaims any responsibility for them.

Any people depicted in stock imagery provided by Getty Images are models, and such images are being used for illustrative purposes only. Certain stock imagery © Getty Images.

Scripture quotations taken from The Holy Bible, New International Version® NIV® Copyright © 1973 1978 1984 2011 by Biblica, Inc. TM. Used by permission. All rights reserved worldwide.

Scripture taken from the New King James Version® Copyright © 1982 by Thomas Nelson. Used by permission. All rights reserved.

ISBN: 978-1-6642-0447-8 (sc)
ISBN: 978-1-6642-0446-1 (e)

Library of Congress Control Number: 2020922678

Print information available on the last page.

WestBow Press rev. date: 11/16/2020

"I've enjoyed your honesty and vulnerability in sharing your story. Inspiring! Encouraging!"
Katherine Hopkins

"Kelly's raw childlike faith is so evident in her honesty! Her love for Jesus and seeking to know and trust Him is challenging me!"
Robin Gwatkin

"Kelly R. Henley has such a unique gift for communication. 'We Will Follow' perfectly blends honesty, humor, and heart."
Corissa Snyder

"Kelly is an example of a transformed life by God's saving grace!!! Her honesty and transparency is encouraging to us all. To God be the glory for all He has done!!!"
Jerry Goss

"Kelly speaks power through her honest, down to earth writing."
Cherri Wheeler

"Kelly's raw and truthful way of telling her story has been such an inspiration to me. She spurs me on to deepen my faith in Jesus through meaningful relationships within my church community."
Amanda Dodd

"Kelly's style of writing is refreshing, witty, and even comical. An amazing testimony of hope and trust. Kelly shares with others just how obtainable a true relationship with God can be."
Tabitha Schmitt

1 Thessalonians 5:11 Therefore encourage one another and build each other up, just as in fact you are doing.

Introduction

Hello, if you're not familiar with our family from our first book We Will Follow let me introduce us. We are the Henley family. My name is Kelly. People like to tell me they enjoy how real I am. How I don't put on a show or try to be fake. You'll hear our story from my perspective. So, please don't expect to only hear about the good times. Sometimes life is hard. Even as a Christian.

I am married to Bubba. He's the perfect person to keep me in line and lead our family. Often having to point out my realness was actually rude and I need to apologize to the person I was "real" with. We have two children Nadia and David. Together we make a great team. We hope you are encouraged as you journey along with us. We pray you see even when life gets hard we can still find victory.

Picking up where We Will Follow ended. You'll get the opportunity to come along side our family as we continue navigating this world with Jesus by our side. You'll witness how fear and insecurity begin to no longer have center stage in our story. We have a calling on our lives and we're determined to fight the strongholds put in place long ago by the enemy. To be honest sometimes it hurts, sometimes we're afraid, and often times we don't understand. But we won't give up, we won't stop following, and we won't stop trusting.

Philippians 1:9-12 And this is my prayer: that your love may abound more and more in knowledge and depth of insight, so that you may be able to discern what is best and may be pure and blameless for the day of Christ, filled with the fruit of righteousness that comes through Jesus Christ- to the glory and praise of God.

Chapter 1

I felt crushed by the pressure of finishing the final stages. I only see the ways I'm capable of messing this up. My stronghold- I doubt often He could actually use me or would want to.

I know He doesn't make mistakes. I know He meant to choose me. Do I believe I'm actually capable? No, I don't. Do I believe He is capable? Without a doubt, yes! Do I sometimes feel He should have chosen someone else? Unfortunately, yes. Chosen someone who didn't spend the whole week stressing. Trying to make sure everything was just right. While not opening her own Bible once! Chosen someone who hasn't been at a breaking point all week. Yet, instead of surrendering she held strong. Chosen someone who isn't in the very strongholds she was years ago.

It's true God uses the weak. Does it mean *I* feel strong while being used? No. It's true God doesn't call the qualified He qualifies the called. Does it mean *I* feel qualified? No.

I have enough faith to know I will obey. I won't give up. I will do this. I will tell our story. I will tell of His faithfulness. I will share my heart for the local church. I will share of His goodness. But being at a place where only God can come through, hurts.

The funny thing is I feel better now. Yes, right now curled up in a ball. Worn out from a major, ugly crying session. This feeling is better *than I've felt all week as little miss tough girl. A tough girl holding it all together. The plates I was balancing just came crashing down. Truth was they were never mine to hold in the first place. He knows what I need to do. He wants to help me. Yet, all week I snatched them from Him. While saying, "You called me. So, I can do this."*

No! He can do it. All He wants me to do is let go. To just let Him lead. I was never meant to carry this load. I was never meant to lead.

All my efforts had been exhausted. There was nothing else I could do. The excruciating pain of trying to hold it altogether had been easier than surrendering. How had I found myself at this place again? A desperate place where I had fought hard to get to.

1 Corinthians 1:26-27 Brothers and sisters, think of what you were when you were called. Not many of you were wise by human standards; not many were influential; not many were of noble birth. But God chose the foolish things of the world to shame the wise; God chose the weak things of the world to shame the strong.

Chapter 2

One of my mentors from the beach mentioned I should write a book. "Yeah, right," I thought. Though I couldn't help wondering, "Is she serious?" She'd read the posts I'd written. Could she really think I had the skills to write a book? "She's probably just being nice," I'd tell myself. Though, she wasn't the type to just blurt out random stuff.

As Christians we have to be careful not to just blurt out everything we feel. Someone may actually be listening to us. We need to give our thoughts a bit more time before escaping our mouths. Giving the Holy Spirit a chance to check them before they enter the world.

Was there any merit to what she'd said? After all I'd noticed a lot of comments on the posts. "We just moved across the country though. They would have commented on anything. They just missed us," I assured myself.

Not all posts had I felt the Spirit before posting. Some were simply updating family. Were the ones He led me to write actually having a larger response? I printed out all the posts along with the comments. Wanting to know if there was a pattern.

The evidence was overwhelming! There was no denying the

posts He led me to write had a larger response. Also people were opening up about their own struggles. He was using me! Was God behind her statement about me writing a book? Could that really be something He would ask me to do? For real, me?

What would people think? Don't people who write books go to college for that kind of stuff? At the very least want to write a book? I decided to pray about it. I wasn't quite sure if He was asking me to write a book or not. Though I knew enough not to just brush this off. I prayed, "Lord, if you want me to write a book I will. But I really don't think this is a good idea."

"Ok good, I'm covered," I thought. If He wants me to write one, He will confirm it, and I will. If He doesn't want me to I will probably just forget about it. A big indicator this was just an idea and God was not behind it.

Over the years I've been taught it's important to reach out to others for prayer. Women I trust to be faithful in their prayers. Anything to do with God is a big deal and should be taken seriously. I also didn't have time to run around doing what people say I should. I want to do what He says. Even if I don't like some of His ideas.

I encourage you to look around in the church. I am not referring to just your church building either. The church refers to the body of believers. The actual people in the churches. Some of the women I'm closest to attend different churches. Seek out people you trust. Ones that believe the truth about God. Preferably ones that know more about faith than you. Not just who have been Christians longer. Longer sometimes doesn't mean anything. Make sure their lives match up to what they are saying. When you find them look to them as an example. Call on them when you need prayer, advice, and a friend. These believers will be invaluable to you as you learn to walk this life with Jesus.

Be careful seeking guidance and advice from non-believers. If you are truly trying to grow closer to God. Why would you follow the directions of those not following God? Where do you think they will lead you? If the person you are seeking advice from isn't going in the same direction as you. Ask yourself, "Where will they lead me?"

This is also true for other Christians. Don't look up to and seek advice from Christians that are not actually living a life that reflects Jesus. We should be striving every day to be more and more like Jesus. Will we mess up? Sure. Will we all let someone down eventually? Sure. But if we are actually following Jesus there should be evidence of our faith in our lives. Simply going to church is not enough evidence. The Bible says the fruits of the Spirit will be evident.

Seek God about who to look to for guidance. It will probably be obvious who you shouldn't look to. Use them as an example of what not to do and move on. Don't condemn them. Don't focus on them. Pray for them. Sometimes people can know all about Jesus and still refuse to allow Him to change their character. We have to do what the Bible says. We have to live it out. Not just hear it. We have to allow Him to change our character. Remember even the religious leaders in the Bible knew a lot about Jesus. But they were nothing like Him in their actions.

James 1:22 Do not merely listen to the word, and so deceive yourselves. Do what it says.

Chapter 3

I continued seeking Him for an answer and continued to ask for prayers. A week or two had gone by and still no confirmations. "Good, must've just been her idea," I thought. I also continued writing the posts. The comments and responses on the inspired posts were definitely pointing to the fact He was using me to encourage others. Even showing them the importance of being transparent about their own struggles.

Why hide stuff? Why pretend it's not happening or hasn't happened? It did. You lived it. I guarantee you aren't the only one. Sometimes all it takes to have a breakthrough is to know we aren't alone. If the enemy can keep us alone. He can convince us we are the only one with these struggles. Wrong! That is a total lie! I promise you someone else is struggling in a very similar way as you. The enemy just wants to keep you in the dark.

I began to feel comfortable enough in the ladies Bible study to share some of our current struggles. I began to get the same reactions I'd get in Mom's Group. Some women seeming unsure how to handle me. Not sure how to handle the blunt honesty.

I still remember that day in Mom's group at the beach. Hearing those moms openly share. The victory I experienced that day, simply by not feeling alone, is the reason I choose to be so transparent. We all have the ability to help others.

During our ladies Bible study the lesson was about being still. About spending time with God. Cutting time out of our busy schedules for Him, allowing Him to speak to us, and to work in our lives. As I listened I couldn't help but think about my season of hand washing clothes. The time spent at the washing station had helped me seek His direction. Helped me hear Him as He guided us towards east Texas.

The discussion time had not allotted for me to share with the whole class. So, I decided to approach one of the leaders after class. To tell her about the washing station. Telling her how the washer and dryer had busted before our mission trip to Kentucky. The funds were not available to get new machines. So we decided to hand wash our clothes. After all, I'd always been intrigued with homesteading. On that mission trip God had clearly told us it was time to leave the beach. Although He hadn't told us where we'd be going. I went on to tell her how I'd spent the next five months handwashing our clothes, praying, and seeking God on the biggest decision of our lives. We searched many states, we pursued many houses, and we lost just as many. All while washing clothes by hand. Loving every minute of the time spent doing it. I depended on that time. After beginning to look into east Texas the desire to hand wash was gone. We had received our answer.

As I finished my story her face expression shocked me. I guess it may have been my nonchalant recount of our story. To me it wasn't that big of a deal anymore. I mean, it was when I was living it. It was the hardest, scariest, and most uncertain time of our lives. But now I already knew how it worked out. Now I was over it. I was just sharing because it had to do with our lesson about being still. Then she said the words I did not want to hear, "You should really write a book."

I left that building knowing exactly what I had to do. Knowing exactly what I didn't want to do. There was no way I was qualified to write a book. What was He trying to do? This is nuts! But I knew enough about God to know He knew what He was doing. Even if I didn't like His idea one bit.

Ephesians 2:10 For we are God's handiwork, created in Christ Jesus to do good works, which God prepared in advance for us to do.

Chapter 4

I knew exactly what He was telling me to do. But everything in me was saying I was the wrong person for the job. A few weeks had went by since that night at Bible study. I hadn't started writing. I was waiting. Maybe He would change His mind. But deep down I knew better. He would not change His mind. No matter how many times I changed mine.

Do you know what had me the most distraught about this idea? Knowing I would have to admit to family and friends I'd written a book. I'm talking about the folks that knew me before Jesus got a hold of me. What would they say? How could I explain that I, unqualified Kelly, had written a book? It's unbelievable how the opinion of a few can outweigh the opinion of many. Or how the opinion of any can outweigh God's.

The day came when I couldn't take it any longer. I knew what He was telling me to do and I was disobeying a direct order. "What harm could come if I just started writing? Maybe He will realize He picked the wrong person," I thought.

The next day I'd wake up before the kids and start writing. "It's our story. It's not like I don't know it. Can't be that hard. I can do this," I coached myself.

I began writing. Quickly had hundreds of words with ease. This was kind of fun. After all I have an amazing memory for random details. I never thought it would come in handy. I can often remember word for word conversations from years ago. The more I wrote the more details I remembered. Looking at the clock I realized I'd been writing four hours straight. Wow, this wasn't as hard as I expected!

I began to write about our first mission trip to Colorado. Nadia interrupts by running in the door excited after checking the mail. Keep in mind she is fifteen. When your teenager is excited after checking the mail it gets your attention. There was a letter from Pastor at the beach. We were both shocked. Pastor doesn't send random letters. I'm pretty sure this was the first letter from him. We'd been living in east Texas for seven months already. I stopped typing and opened the letter. In the letter was a photo of us. A photo from our first mission trip in Colorado. It even had the tack holes from the bulletin board at church.

Tears began to run down my cheeks. "God, he had no reason to send this to us. He knew we had a bunch of these." In that moment I knew this was God's confirmation. He was calling me to write a book. A real one.

Not only had God laid it on Pastor's heart to take the photo off the board. Having him send it to us. But God also planned for it to arrive when I was in the middle of typing the very first sentence about the Colorado mission trip. When those types of confirmations come my way I need to decide. Is my fear of rejection bigger than my God? Will I allow my fear to direct me? Will I trust that God knows what He's doing? I will trust Him. I will do what He says. Even if I'm scared.

Sometimes I sit and remember a time when I believed life

was just random chance and coincidence. The haphazardness I'd always felt was normal. Living in a world of good luck and bad luck. I know it's many others' normal still. If something happens there is no expectation of reason. It is just a random coincidence.

The closer you get to God and the more you grow in your faith you'll realize nothing is a coincidence. It would've been a much further stretch for me to believe so many coincidences took place for that photo to be in my hand. Right as I typed that sentence.

For real. Let's walk through what those coincidences may have looked like. Granted I need it to be clear. It was not a coincidence. It was God. But let's walk through what I would have accepted before. *Pastor let's say seven days ago. Walks near the bulletin board for probably the hundredth time this month. Sees the photo that's been there almost two years. He takes it down. Decides, "Hey let's mail this to the Henleys." Keep in mind he knew we had more of them. After all we'd given him the photo in the first place. Returns to his desk. Writes a letter to us. Gets the letter to the church office to be mailed. It gets mailed on the exact day it needs to. Ends up at our post office on the right day. Our mail lady shows up and Nadia checks it. She hands me the letter at the exact moment I'm writing the sentence about our mission trip. When that photo was taken in the first place.*

How many "coincidences" have to line up perfectly before some of you will admit that someone is in charge? I have seen God work in the past. All I had to do was see that photo and I knew God had orchestrated it all. All because He cared enough to know I needed a little extra push. I needed to be sure He was telling me to do this.

You don't live in a world full of random chance and coincidences. It would actually take a lot less effort and just a little faith for you to see and admit that someone is in charge. And I promise it's not you. Even if you think it's you because you don't believe in God. Than you probably are still choosing to follow luck, chance, and superstition. Even in your life without God you still don't think you're in charge.

There is a peace and security that comes with knowing we aren't in charge because a caring, personal God is. This is something the world cannot offer. When we try to find peace and security in things this world has to offer it is only temporary.

Now I can simply say and believe, "God is in control. He knows what is going on. This may seem bad now, but He can work even this for my good. I will trust Him. He loves me and has a great plan for my life." I no longer believe the illusion of being in charge or in control of my life. It actually feels pretty great to know someone bigger and more powerful has got me in His hands. He cares about all of us.

I may not always feel like the most trusting Christian on the block. But in my heart I know I believe that God is in control. As my faith grows I will trust more without my feelings getting a say.

1 Corinthians 2:13-14 This is what we speak, not in words taught us by human wisdom but in words taught by the Spirit, explaining spiritual realities with Spirit-taught words. The person without the Spirit does not accept the things that come from the Spirit of God but considers them foolishness, and cannot understand them because they are discerned only through the Spirit

Chapter 5

Each day I woke up before the kids and wrote. After five days I was done. With seventeen chapters our story was written. I'd written mainly about how God directed us to east Texas. Although I did add how our family came to know who God was. Relevant because why else would we pack up our family if we hadn't known how huge our God was. Other than correcting grammar it was done. Most of what I read online said editing was the publisher's job anyway. Good thing, because I don't know what I'm doing.

I wondered why it seemed to take other people so long to write a book. Some articles online said it took years. That's crazy! Well, God told me to write mine. Maybe that's why mine was written so fast. Whenever I'm acting this arrogant it should be my first clue I'm doing something wrong. Yet, I don't realize it. Not yet at least. Thankfully I'm always growing and we have a very patient God.

As I'd read over the manuscript I could tell something was missing. I wasn't sure what it was. But something definitely wasn't right. It wasn't like the posts. I did what He'd said. I wrote a book. About our story.

Days went on and I'd read it again. Something was still missing. I began to pray. Asking God what I'd done wrong. "I did what you said. I wrote our story. I tried to tell you I wasn't qualified," I continued praying. While rereading the story over and over again.

I began to see clearly what He was showing me. I'd written nothing more than a timeline. I'd simply stated what happened and moved on. The posts were full of emotion. Full of the true feelings I had at the time while writing them. "Ok God, I understand what you're saying. But the problem is I already lived this. It's over. It's in the past. I already know what happens. Dude, it doesn't hurt anymore."

As I continued to pray. My prayers began to change to, "Help me feel what I felt." This prayer was an innocent yet powerful prayer. When we get our prayers lined up with His will it's amazing to see the power of our God.

I began at the beginning. He was faithful to hold up His end of the bargain. As each event came up I felt what I'd felt. I felt the joy, the fear, and the hurt. The raw emotions left me exhausted many days. Most days I'd spend crying. Not even aware certain seasons had been so hard on me. As I'd read back over an event I would cry again and again. Until it didn't hurt anymore. God was healing my hurts through the book He asked me to write.

Sometimes it took weeks to rewrite a section. Depending on how rough that season had been. I was amazed how often lessons we'd learned came up in Bible study. Giving me the opportunity to share. I wouldn't have been able to share the raw, honest emotions had I not relived them that very morning.

I began writing in March. By July I felt I was finished. This may not seem like a long time. But for me this was excruciating.

Not only was I reliving some of the hardest things I'd ever gone through but Bubba was still working out of town.

We loved our new church. We had the opportunity to be involved in many outreaches. Yet, I wasn't signing up for any. When Bubba was home we spent all our time with him. Not knowing how long he'd be with us. We also had the opportunity to travel with him. Sometimes only getting a day's notice. In my eyes it didn't matter what other plans we had. We would choose him. Which meant we needed to always be available to leave. I chose not to volunteer or sign up for anything. That way we wouldn't let anyone else down.

I attended church faithfully. Yet, it had been almost a year since I'd served in a local church. "Must just be part of the season we are in. Maybe the book is my new service," I'd think to myself. I did prefer to be home when Bubba was gone. I hated the idea of doing things without him. We'd always done everything together.

It was obvious I was only living when he was home. I'd fill my time with a few activities here and there while he was gone. It was all just to pass the time until he returned. I could handle the trips that lasted only a few days. I'd spend my days getting all my house chores accomplished. That way I could focus on him when he returned. It was easy to keep myself busy for a few days.

When he was gone for longer stretches it became obvious I had a problem. I had no motivation to do anything and I'd cry at a moment's notice. The days before he left I would cause fights between us. The result of being so upset. Ruining the few days together we had with him. He'd leave and the guilt from fighting would take over. I didn't want to do anything but stay in bed. Feeling horrible for the way I'd acted. With days until his return I'd pull myself together. Focusing on the house chores I'd let go.

I wasn't living. Why had God sent us here for this? Why had He moved us here to go through this? Just for the book! That didn't seem fair! I wanted my family back! My feelings were controlling me. I needed to find God's truth. I wasn't acting like I trusted Him.

2 Corinthians 4:8-9 We are hard pressed on every side, but not crushed; perplexed, but not in despair; persecuted, but not abandoned; struck down, but not destroyed.

Chapter 6

Bubba asked me to mow the grass while he was away. He'd taught me how to use the mower. "This won't be a problem. I can handle it," I assured him. Although I had no idea what I was doing. Everything was fine until I actually tried to pull the mower out of the shed. That's when I hit the deck on the door. I hit it real hard. After getting it all the way out, I started it up, and it was rattling. I definitely didn't remember it making that noise. At this point I'm pretty sure if I try to mow the blade will fly off, chopping off my leg, or one of my children's legs. Nope, not doing it. While trying to get the mower back in the shed I accidently whacked it on the door again. This was really not good.

Bubba wouldn't be home for a few weeks this time. I had to figure out how to mow the grass. I decided to ask in Sunday school if anyone knew any numbers for lawn guys. After all I'm at home alone with the kids. I didn't need some potential creeper at my house mowing my grass. Maybe they would know a number for a nice/safe company.

Up until this point I'd only reached out to the beach for help. I didn't think I could open up in Sunday school about our problems. I was trying to pull off a tough girl act. When in reality I was losing it. I experienced a lot of healing by just simply confessing what I was going through to the class. I should've recognized the enemy's tactic of keeping me silent. If I kept silent about my current struggles the people here had no chance to help me. They only knew what I was willing to share.

After explaining what happened I was blown away by how eager they were to help. Multiple people offering to mow the lawn for us. The next day two men from the church along with their families came. They mowed and visited with us. That day meant a lot to us.

In this act of kindness we realized we can rely on our new church family just as much as we could our old church family. Come to find out the mower wasn't broken at all and the rattle was normal. I'm so thankful I thought it was broken.

Unless you're willing to admit you're having a problem you'll never know who God would use to help you. I was having a problem. Well, a lot of problems but on that particular Sunday I was having a lawn problem. To the men with trailers and mowers it wasn't a big deal at all. To me it was. For me this problem ran much deeper. My problem; my husband was gone. My husband who was supposed to be here, wasn't. I didn't want to mow because it meant he couldn't. I felt alone. I felt isolated. Yes, I may have been completely overreacting but that's how I felt. I was in a new town, a new church, no homeschool group, and my husband was gone.

Through the churches actions that day I realized I wasn't alone. I hadn't been alone. I'd simply isolated myself. Preventing anyone from coming along side of my family and helping.

If you need help or prayer just ask. People are waiting to help you. You just haven't given them the chance. As followers we are not called to be tough and struggle alone. We are asked to lean on each other.

Hebrews 6:10 God is not unjust; he will not forget your work and the love you have shown him as you have helped his people and continue to help them.

Chapter 7

Bubba's job was crushing me. I needed to find God's truth in these circumstances. God's truth stated I shouldn't try to find my joy, peace, and comfort in Bubba. I should find them in God and God alone. If I truly found my joy, peace, and comfort in God than I'd be ok if Bubba weren't here. I'd still miss him. But I wouldn't be crushed by his absence.

As I wrote each morning I was reminded of how faithful God is. How in control He is. Reminded of the fact that He knows what's going on and will work all things for good. Even if they don't seem good right now. I needed these constant daily reminders of just how big of a God we serve.

The kids and I attended a fellowship with our Sunday school class. I didn't want to go without Bubba. But I knew this would be a great first step in choosing to live while he was gone. That night I told him all about our evening. For the first time I realized how much this was effecting him. He'd wanted to be there too.

Not once had I stopped to think about how this was effecting him. I wasn't thinking about how for the first time since being a husband and father he was away from his wife and children. I wasn't thinking about how every night after he called us he'd sit in a hotel room, alone. Not only was he working through all of his own emotions. He had to deal with me and all of mine. And I wasn't handling this well at all. If I felt upset about him not being able to mow the grass. Imagine how he felt. He'd always been here. He'd always handled this kind of stuff. How selfish I'd been over the last few months. He was doing the best he could to provide for us and I was acting like it was killing me.

This reminded me of when I learned our husbands aren't meant to be our entire social circles. We cannot expect them to fill all those shoes. Now I was expecting him to be my source of joy, peace, safety, and comfort. Completely setting him up for failure. That is not his job. Only God is capable of being my source of joy. Only God is capable of providing peace in the midst of crazy circumstances. Only God is capable of protecting us. And only God is capable of comforting me when things are not going the way I expected or planned. No wonder I was a wreck every time Bubba left. All this time I'd been relying on him to do what only God could do.

Isaiah 58:11 The LORD *will guide you always; he will satisfy your needs in a sun-scorched land and will strengthen your frame. You will be like a well-watered garden, like a spring whose waters never fail.*

Chapter 8

Vacation Bible School was quickly approaching. Beforehand they were going to pass out flyers around the neighborhood. Inviting local families. I'd done this before and I was definitely not going to make the same mistake I'd made before. Sometimes I look back and can't imagine what I was thinking. Before our fall festival at the beach I'd had an idea to hand out similar flyers to local families. Simply wanting people to know they were really invited. That it wasn't just an event for church people. A week before the event the kids and I set out to distribute the invitations.

As the day arrived I was ready for an amazing time. Fully decked out in my Tinker Bell costume. The flyers weren't even on my mind. The event started and people started coming. I recognized them from the neighborhood. They kept coming and coming. I was in complete shock. The more excited I got, the more pressure I felt, and then I lost all self-control. I took my eyes off God completely.

If only I'd had the faith to know God brought them to the church that day. I wouldn't have had the attitude of, "They are here because of me. So I have to do everything in my power to make them come back." All I accomplished was completely scaring off about forty people. People who'd just given church a chance. Because of an invitation they received from a Christian. Who probably seemed sane when she gave it to them. They showed up to find a spaz in a Tinker Bell suit. Let's just leave it at none of them came back the next week.

I have enough faith now to know I didn't mess up God's plan for their lives. I assure you, I'm not powerful enough to mess up His plans. He simply would have used someone else. Someone else would have received the blessing of watching a family find freedom. The kind only Jesus can offer.

The lessons I learned through that fall festival forever changed my life. God brought those people to that festival. He was more than capable of bringing them back. My job was to love them. To be excited to see them. But not scary excited. And then to invite them back. Instead of trying to micromanage Jesus. Literally scaring them off. It takes a lot of self-control to not seem overbearing. Especially, when I know what is potentially around the corner for someone. I know what a life given to Jesus looks like. I know the victory and freedom that can be found. But now I also know His timing is perfect. His divine appointments of people and places is where the miracles happen.

The excitement I feel has to be given to Him. I have to step back and say, "It's you God. They showed up because of You. Ultimately You decide if this is the time they say yes." Often this prayer is followed with me begging, "Please don't let me mess this up. If you know I will mess this up than don't let me show up at all." He's been faithful. The hardest part is having to just say, "I trust you." Even when they still don't come back.

He also taught me that having "all are welcome" on your marquee is not enough. Sometimes people really need you to invite them personally. Sometimes people need to know, "I am welcome." Not just, "All are welcome."

John 6:44 "No one can come to me unless the Father who sent me draws them, and I will raise them up at the last day."

Chapter 9

I wanted to sign up and help with Vacation Bible School. I loved helping with this type of stuff. As it approached I realized I was terrified. How could I be scared? There weren't many people I was comfortable telling I was afraid.

It took days to work up enough courage to ask for help. Being careful to word it in such a way that it was obvious I didn't want to feel this way. I didn't want to avoid church stuff. I didn't want to stay home. I wanted my old self back. I wanted the girl that loved all things church. The following is the actual text exchange. As you read this I pray you find women you can call on in times of need. Women who will be transparent and honest with you. Who will use their own struggles to help you in yours?

"I need some clarity, sanity, or something that you normally have to offer. I haven't signed up to help with anything at church. Mainly because of our life. I feel so unreliable. I don't want to commit to anything.

So this week I want to help on Wednesday to hand out flyers for VBS. And for two days I want to help with VBS. I am so nervous. I can't even think about handing the flyers out without feeling super overwhelmed. To the point I don't want to go. What is wrong with me? I love serving.

All I can reason is that I'm barely keeping my head above the water as is. Adding more is setting me over the edge. Or is Satan just being dumb?"

Her reply to me-"Hey Kelly! Well first let me say I can totally relate. For years I loved to share with women and lead Bible studies. Then as we had more children (and moved across the country) life got busy. My leadership took a backseat. It was necessary. But then it became an excuse. And then I became afraid.

And so when the opportunities would arise. I would justify that I was barely staying afloat myself and couldn't take on more. It was true. But it became something I hid behind. And as time went on, I became more comfortable at home and less comfortable serving and leading. Until I realized that even the idea of stepping back in paralyzed me with fear. I no longer felt capable.

And then one day, our church back in CA called and asked me to fly out and speak at their women's retreat. I was pregnant with number four and thought, 'No way! My hands are way too full and my brain doesn't even work anymore.' It seemed so ironic that they would want me to come. They had access to countless more qualified women. I couldn't help but think, maybe this is God. I asked my mentor what she thought. Hoping she would agree that I was too busy and the timing was bad. But she said, 'Do it afraid.' Not what I wanted to hear. But in my heart I knew she was right.

I was terrified. I felt inadequate, under-qualified, and I was pretty sure that if Jesus didn't come back beforehand I would die when I took the mic. Jesus did not come back, even though I begged. And I was afraid until the moment I stepped up there. But when I did an amazing thing happened. Something broke in the Spirit realm and suddenly I was not afraid. I was empowered. He set me free in a big way through that small act of obedience. It was life changing for me." As I read her reply I knew what I had to do. I had to, "Do it afraid."

Psalm 56:3 When I am afraid, I put my trust in you

Chapter 10

Over the last few weeks I'd been researching a few publishers. I wanted to go with a Christian publisher. After all I had no idea what I was doing. Having an honest company to work with would be the best choice. Least that way I wouldn't be taken advantage of. I researched Christian publishers online. There were a lot more than I expected. I'd read through what the different ones offered. I had no idea what I was looking for in a publisher.

God already knew which company I needed to go with. We prayed over and continued learning about each company. After doing our best to follow His direction we chose one. The next thing I needed to do was go to their website and fill out the little information form. No harm in that. They'll just send me an information packet in the mail.

Finally I got up enough courage to fill out the form. I felt like I was going to get sick. This was horrible. "It's just a form online. Get yourself together," I told myself. "OK I can do this." I open up the form and the second question ruins all my bravery. "What are your goals for your book?" Ummm. I don't have any! I didn't want to write it! This was not even my plan. They didn't have an option for, "God told me to." Come on y'all! This is a Christian company. Don't a lot of Christians do things just because, "God told them to."

I had to choose one of their options. "Sharing my story with family and friends." Nope, not that one. That was my biggest fear. "Writing to help others overcome a personal obstacle." No, this was our story not theirs. "Writing about my hobby or personal passion." Jesus is definitely not a hobby. A big no for that one! "Sharing Information on a specialized topic." Kind of think this one would work. "Expressing my deepest thought." No, that sounds way too fancy. "Writing to reach a wide circle of readers." I did want non-believers to understand it also. "I write poetry and want to share my poetry with others." No, I do not "want" to share what I wrote with anyone. "Writing for fame," I'm pretty sure that one must be a joke.

It was a toss-up between, "Sharing information on a specialized topic and writing to reach a wide circle of people." I had to decide which was more important to me. Sharing information or reaching people? I knew right away reaching people should always be our goal. That would be my choice. What was supposed to be a simple online form turned into a huge endeavor. How had I not even asked myself the question of why? I finished the questions and pressed send. Good, glad that was over!

Less than two minutes later the phone rings. It's them! The publishing company! Nope, this was not my plan. They were not supposed to call me. This was supposed to be a packet that came in the mail in a few weeks. I was already a wreck from just filling out their form.

I fumbled through the call. The guy on the other end found out he'd just called someone who had no idea what they were talking about. He asked me, "Why did you want to write the book?" I replied, "I did not want to write the book. I had no intention of ever writing a book in my life." The surprise in his voice was pretty hilarious. I continued explaining, "Until March I had no idea I would ever be doing this. I don't think this is a good idea at all. But my feelings are irrelevant. So I wrote the book." I explained to him how nervous I was. He assured me, "All first time authors are nervous." "Dude, I'm not an author," I replied.

Ephesians 2:10 For we are God's handiwork, created in Christ Jesus to do good works, which God prepared in advance for us to do.

Chapter 11

I was definitely in the middle of a confidence crisis about being an author. Bubba was about to leave for weeks, VBS was approaching, and we were preparing to drive to Ohio. To meet him on a job. On a positive note my Mom moved to east Texas six months after us. With her here east Texas wasn't as lonely. She planned on riding to Ohio with the kids and I. Making it a little less scary.

I was terrified of everything having to do with the trip to Ohio. Even though Bubba had preprogramed the whole trip on the GPS. The only thing I needed to do was figure out where to stop and get gas. He'd already made it clear we could only stop at nice truck stops or nice rest areas. There would be no stopping at creepy gas stations.

This season was more about getting me out of my comfort zone than I'd like to admit. I often feel like I'm painting a horrible picture of being a Christian. Simply because I'm constantly having problems. As you can tell I do not like change. Nor do I handle it very well at all. God was pushing us all to our limits. I seemed to be fighting tooth and nail for control. Grasping at any false sense of security I could find.

I've shared before and I'll share again. Majority of my problems are my inability to let go of control. God has brought our family to and through some amazing circumstances. They've shaped and molded us for the better. In so many ways.

He's removed toxic relationships from our lives. Replacing those with life giving relationships. He has removed strongholds. Replacing those with a passion to lead others to His truth. Life as a Christian is not easy but it's amazing and has purpose.

Alright, back to our ever changing story. The day of VBS comes and I walk in repeating to myself, "Just do it afraid. Just do it afraid." The music starts and I am ok. Actually I feel amazing. This is who I am. I'm a server. Fear had controlled me and consumed me. This is why she said, "Do it afraid." All I had to do was push through the fear and God could do the rest.

Many women from the church checked on me. Wanting to see how I was doing. I was great. I was me again. The chains of fear had broken. They were gone as soon as the music started. I knew I'd be ok to drive to Ohio. I could just do it afraid. Fear didn't need to control me.

We started our drive to Ohio. Everyone seemed confident we could handle this. All was going well. We had prayed a lot and asked lots of people for prayer. We'd traveled so much we felt we were a pretty well-oiled machine. Just missing one person this time.

Everything was going fine until we made our first stop. We'd already decided either Mom or I would wait outside of the men's room for David to come out. This way he wasn't standing outside the door alone. Trafficking is real and I'm not playing around. Mom heads into the girl's room with Nadia and I send David into the men's room. Each time the door swings open I see him just standing in the middle of the room, not moving. "Maybe he's waiting in line or something," I think to myself. The door opens again and he's still standing there. What is going on? I open the door and call to him to come to me. He turns to look at me, pale faced, and walks out. I ask him, "What's going on?" He tells me, "I left my knife in the car. Dad says I should always carry a pocket knife." I reassure him that it's ok and we will go get his knife. After getting the knife we all used the restroom.

Getting in line to pay for our items, my son won't walk. I can see his hands shaking and he won't move to the counter. I ask him, "What's going on?" He looks at me with the same face I saw in the bathroom and says, "This is the first stop we've ever made without Dad. Dad protects us." Fear was controlling him. Before this trip could continue we needed some help. We prayed in the parking lot and called Bubba. I needed his help to reassure him that we were safe.

During the phone call Bubba told him, "All along it had been God who had kept us safe." We all needed to rely on God's provision and protection more than we relied on Bubba. I also needed to face the fact my inability to function without fear was rubbing off on my kids. I needed to find a way to believe God's truth more than my feelings.

Fear can be a crushing feeling. Only with God's help can we truly overcome fear. Fear does not need to control us. Nor should we be content with living in fear. From then on David was ok. He knew God was with him and Dad. Protecting them both.

After meeting Bubba in Ohio we'd planned to head back to the beach to visit family and help with Kitty Hawk's VBS. I also planned to go to our old house for the first time since leaving. I'd refused to go back to that house after we left. I'd been feeling in the last few months that God wanted me to face my fear and hurt. I contacted my friend (the new owner) and asked if I could stop by.

If you're thinking, "Why do it if you don't want to?" Well, the cool thing about being a follower is you don't really need to understand. You just obey. I didn't know why I needed to do this. Most of the time I don't know why He asks me to do things. But I will listen and obey nonetheless. Majority of the time a victory of some sort is right around the corner of obedience.

Ok, back to our journey. The day arrived when I'd go to the house. I'd been dreading this day for over a year now. I pulled down the street I'd driven down so many times. I felt nothing. As I pulled in and parked behind her car. It felt strange but it didn't hurt. I was so familiar with this yard yet it didn't feel like mine anymore. I walked up the steps, knocked, and went into the house. This place didn't feel like my home. My security wasn't found in a home anymore. My security was found in God.

This is why God wanted me to go. I was dreading a hurt that no longer existed. It was simply a shadow of what once hurt. I wasn't the same person anymore. My hope and security weren't found in memories anymore. I was growing. Had I not obeyed and went, even though I didn't want to, I wouldn't have found this victory.

Psalm 33:20-22 We put our hope in the LORD. He is our help and our shield. In him our hearts rejoice, for we trust in his holy name. Let your unfailing love surround us, LORD, for our hope is in you alone. NLT

Chapter 12

I didn't plan to tell anyone at the beach I'd written a book. This would stay our little secret until it was necessary for people to know. I couldn't face the doubts, the reactions, and the questions. A few people from the church knew and that was it.

I thought my unwillingness to tell everyone was my lack of confidence. Which did play a part but looking back it was much more. I needed to work through what God was calling me to. At this point I was still doubting. Just like when we were told to leave the beach. It was important we spent time with God before we told everyone. Seeking Him until we believed in our hearts what He was calling us to. If we'd ran around telling everyone, when we were unsure ourselves, their opinions could have swayed us.

With that said, it's important to reach out to a few trusted followers for godly wisdom and prayer. People you know that will seek God on your behalf. Every random Bob, Joe, and Suzie should not be able to influence your decision to follow God.

At the beach we were able to spend a few days at VBS. On the last day was family time. During that time the parents get to watch the children perform songs from the week.

The years we were at Kitty Hawk Baptist Church many

families had come and gone. Walking into the sanctuary, where the parents were seated, I noticed the missionary from Bible study. Whom I look up to very much. I ran to sit near her. Feeling grateful I got to see her on this trip. As we watched Pastor get the kids worked up over the offering reaching the goal. I was overwhelmed as I recalled my very first VBS. Before I knew who she was or how her service to Jesus would affect my life. Bubba and I had sat in that very sanctuary cheering with the kids as the offering came in. Each year Kitty Hawk took up an offering for a different missionary's need. That first year the offering had been for a Rondavel. A type of house they have in Africa. She was the missionary.

I leaned over with tears in my eyes and said, "I remember doing this for you." As I watched the tears stream down her cheeks I thanked the Lord for this gift He'd offered me through her service. I was a missionary too. On our first mission trip to Colorado she planted a seed when she told me, "You are a missionary now." A seed that took root. We were not just going on a mission trip. We were missionaries.

Looking around the sanctuary I was overwhelmed by the families that were here. Others had come from out of town also. We were all here by the grace of God. I did my best to soak it all in. Not wanting to take one second for granted. Soon enough we'd be heading in our own directions.

After arriving home I received an email from the publisher. It was time to submit the manuscript. This was horrible! Someone I didn't even know was about to read it. They also wanted me to send them a bunch of other stuff. Things like an about the book, about the author, free preview, and keynote. I also needed to choose the page color, size of the book, and the cover design.

"God, you have got to be kidding me! All you told me to do was write a book! I don't even know what most of this stuff is. Did other people know about this stuff?" I allowed my thoughts to spiral into a panic.

I literally cried myself to sleep that night. How could I do this? I didn't even know what this stuff meant. How could I make all these decisions? Why did God ask me? Why couldn't He ask someone else, someone more qualified?

2 Corinthians 12:9 But he said to me, "My grace is sufficient for you, for my power is made perfect in weakness." Therefore I will boast all the more gladly about my weaknesses, so that Christ's power may rest on me.

Chapter 13

Waking up the next day I didn't want to think about the book at all. This was horrible. I'd worked hard to write that manuscript. Now they just wanted more from me. Then the phone rang. It was them! Wanting to know if I'd received their email. I informed them I'd received it and cried all night. I'd get back to them when I figured out what I was going to do.

This was really the first time I realized God knew exactly what company to send me to. They were helpful, patient, and supportive. It was pretty clear to everyone I was a wreck about this whole process. It was clear I had no idea what I was doing. I'm pretty sure they understood I didn't want to do this. I remember how shocked he sounded when he asked if my family and friends were excited. I told him I'd barely told anyone about it.

No matter how much I wanted to quit. I couldn't follow fear. After all I just wrote a book about how hard, scary, and frustrating following God across the country was. All throughout that journey I was reminded constantly of how faithful He is. How I felt never changed who He was. His character and what He'd done for me is why I'd do anything for Him. That included publishing this book. I had to remember, think back to the confirmations, and stand on them. Not on how I was feeling.

First step, I needed to write this stuff down. I grabbed an index card and wrote a list of the items in the email. I began the task of checking them off. About the book was first. I grabbed as many books as we had on the shelf and read the backs of them. Oh wow! They sound super fancy. Pretty much summarizing their whole book in a paragraph or two. Moving on to the next thing on the list. I researched and learned what they expected when they said "about the author." I was supposed to write my credentials and summarize me in third person. Nope, not happening! First off, I don't have credentials. Second, I'm not an author. I decided to read the author parts of the books on our shelves. That was a bad idea. There was no way I could measure up.

I hadn't even given one thought to what the cover of the book would look like. "Why is this happening? Why did He pick me? I don't want to make all these decisions. What if I make the wrong decisions and mess it all up? Lord, do you know how many people you could have asked? They would have already known this stuff. Why me? God, why are you doing this," I cried out!

I needed to stop pouting. Stop wishing things were different. I needed to do what He was calling me to do. If I was relying on Him, even a little bit, I wouldn't be focused on all these details. My circumstances were consuming me. I was trusting my own understanding. I wasn't trusting Him or standing on His truth. The God who created it all, including me, called me to do this. Therefore, He was more than capable of helping me do it.

I was confident He was calling me to do this. I'd sought Him for direction before beginning. I asked others to pray with us. I'd waited for His answer. I'd been quiet to make sure I heard Him.

He'd confirmed in multiple ways He was asking me to do this. Yes me, unqualified Kelly. Yes, the high school dropout. Yes, the former drug addict. If only I could stop seeing me through my past and my failures. If only I could see me the way He does.

Proverbs 3:5-6 Trust in the Lord with all your heart, And lean not on your own understanding; In all your ways acknowledge Him, And He shall direct your paths. NKJV

Chapter 14

Bubba's work had been extremely slow since arriving home from the beach. Giving us the opportunity to spend time together and allowing him to help with the final steps of the manuscript.

We finished all the things they asked. Now the only thing left to do was send it to them. I literally just needed to press send. From the outside it looked pretty simple. For me, this was paralyzing! While completing the submission form I'd made decisions I didn't feel qualified to make. I was terrified of messing this up.

I knew I should let God have control. I should let Him carry the weight. I knew He would see me through this. I knew if He called me He would qualify me. So why wasn't I feeling that way? Why do I always allow my feelings to decide how I respond? Bubba interrupted my spiraling thoughts and said, "Just do it already! Send it!" I pressed send.

Wow, that was ridiculously hard for me! Glad it was over and life can move on. All the information I submitted would be sent to the content department for review. They'd let me know of anything needing approval or permission to publish. That would probably take them awhile. I was thankful I'd have a long break from book stuff.

Wrong! Within a few days I received an email back. How did they read it so fast? I was not ready for their feedback. I spent all day looking at that email notification refusing to open it. Working up enough courage I finally opened it. As I began to read I couldn't believe what I was seeing. I needed to correct my profanity. "What?! Are you kidding me, God? How am I being corrected for profanity while trying to publish a Christian book? God, are you sure you picked the right chick?" When I calmed down and decided to think logically these were easy fixes. After correcting my mistakes I sent the manuscript back. It wasn't as scary this time.

The next step was the editorial assessment. Finally, I would know what kind of editing I needed and the cost. Bubba had still been off work. This was not a good time to tell him I needed more money.

Matthew 6:8 Do not be like them, for your Father knows what you need before you ask him.

Chapter 15

I received an email back only a few days later. I'm really starting to get irritated by how quick they are. I am hoping they won't get back to me for weeks. This process is stressful. This process hurts. Yes, mainly because day in and day out I am grabbing ahold of the reigns and trying to grasp control. Having to lose it and let God lead. While really just trying to enjoy the time Bubba is home. Each time I complete a milestone with the book I sigh a sigh of relief. Happy to receive a break. Wrong, these people are like publishing ninjas!

The email is from the editorial department they have completed the assessment. And I am not clicking on it. Nope. Going to just pretend I never got it. What if they tell me it's horrible? What if they tell me that my story doesn't make sense? What if they tell me nobody cares? Or worse what if they tell me it's good? What if it's successful? What if people want me to talk about it? What if I have to deal with different companies and make different decisions? "Lord, I don't want to do this anymore," I complained. Bubba finds out the email came and tells me to, "Just open it." "Yeah, easy for him to say. His whole life isn't hanging in the balance right now," I whined. Ok, neither was mine. But it surely felt that way.

When I opened the email at the very top was the overall comments from the editor. "I found this to be a warm, uplifting book that mixes memoir and self-help. In it, you chronicle your spiritual journey from not having strong faith in God to believing he is indeed your father. You had doubts, but by studying the Bible, praying, and communing with other Christians, you learned the truth about God. As a result, your book will inspire others to grow in Christ. Your book is filled with important Christian messages."

After reading, I sat in shock. Really? A real editor who doesn't even know me and isn't just being nice thinks it's going to help people. If only I'd let that sink in before moving on to the rest of the email.

They suggested the book needed, "Tighter writing." What is that? They also said, "Do not use all caps but rather small caps." What is a small cap? "Delete verse numbers." Why don't people need to know how to find the verses? "The book does not line up with The Chicago Manual of Style." Who are these people and why do I care if they like my style? And the one simple correction that threw me over the edge, "Bible starts with an uppercase letter." That's it! I'm done! "Lord, I didn't even capitalize Bible in a Christian book! Dude, you got the wrong chick! I'm not doing this anymore! This is crazy!"

Not only was I now completely disqualified from being an author in my own head. They had also sample edited the first 1700 words. Now I didn't even sound like me. I would never talk like that!

I knew what I needed to do to make this successful. I couldn't sound like me. Because me didn't even capitalize Bible and my style was wrong. Now it would be up to God to figure out the finances to cover editing. Because right now God knew we did not have the money. Bubba had still been off work for over a month. I wasn't going to ask him for money.

For the first time since arriving in east Texas Bubba started making connections with the men in the church. He'd started serving on Wednesday nights and Sunday evenings. He'd also been able to join a men's Bible study that met every Friday morning. Each and every time he served he knew he didn't want to leave again. What he didn't know was that I'd started praying. Praying specifically for him.

Philippians 4:6 Do not be anxious about anything, but in every situation, by prayer and petition, with thanksgiving, present your requests to God

Chapter 16

In our ladies group at church we'd started a study on the power of prayer. About how we should fight our battles using God's Word. I'd made it known to God how upset I was about Bubba being gone since he'd started this job. But I wasn't praying. I wasn't trying to get my heart aligned with God. All I was doing was telling God how upset I was that Bubba wasn't here with us. I wanted him home but it was for selfish reasons. I started praying for him to realize this job paid great and had great perks. But this job took him from church.

I began to see over the months a growing desire in Bubba to seek God on his own. He would read scriptures each day in his hotel room. He would watch sermons on the television. He continued to pray with the kids each evening. All of this was great and it was something I'd longed to see for years. But he was still missing the power of the local church. The body of believers that are here to support each other, lean on each other, and help each other grow. We are not called to be lone wolf Christians. Since arriving in east Texas Bubba had only been able to attend church what felt like a handful of times. His schedule was never consistent enough to volunteer or serve.

I continued to learn more in my Bible study about the prayers I should be praying. Learning that I needed to stop fighting the symptoms and find the root of the problem. Bubba's job was not my enemy. There is a real enemy working here. The hardest part, having to admit God may answer by telling me Bubba is called to shine his light on the road. What if God's choice was not me and the kids? What if His answer wasn't what I wanted to hear? Would I still trust Him? Would I still trust that He knew what was best for us?

The scripture I chose to pray is found in 1 Timothy 6:11-12. *But you, man of God. Flee from all this, and pursue righteousness, godliness, faith, love, endurance and gentleness. Fight the good fight of the faith. Take hold of the eternal life to which you were called when you made your good confession in the presence of many witnesses.*

Bubba didn't know I was praying this. I continued faithfully fighting for my husband. Because deep down I didn't know if he was being tempted with the perks or if this was still God's path. I knew it wasn't my job to figure it out. It was my job to go on my husband's behalf and fight for him.

At the moment, I was simply thankful God had given Bubba a break long enough to make some connections with local guys. Maybe His plan would be for Bubba to be home every once in a while to fuel up. Forgetting about the fact that when Bubba was home we had very little income. He had a few odd carpentry jobs here and there. Which were great and held us over. We knew God would provide.

I continued to pray and he continued to be home. Serving and making relationships. Having dinner with new friends from church. Serving as a family was finally happening after a year of being in east Texas. I missed seeing him so happy. The job with all its perks never came close to the happiness and peace I saw on his face while serving.

"If only for a little while, Lord. Thank you for bringing him back to church," I would think as I watched him thriving. My heart was changing. I no longer wanted him home for me. I no longer wanted him home for the kids. I wanted Bubba home for church. For service to God. I'd missed seeing the joy in his face. The joy that only comes from serving the one who gave His all for you. Bubba is a server.

Each evening as a family we would walk around our neighborhood. I loved this time together. On one particular evening Bubba looked at me, "I want to quit my job. Each time I get to serve the more I don't want to leave again. I know we need the money. I don't know why I am feeling this way." Oh man, I hadn't told him about what I was praying. As soon as he said the words, "I don't know why." I pictured my torn out yellow, legal pad paper I'd been using that contained the specific prayers for him.

The Bible study said to be specific and use scriptures. Oh I did, and I'd even cried out on my knees while praying these scriptures over him. I really wondered how mad Bubba was going to be when he found out. He really liked that job. He really liked the traveling, perks, and potential for growth. I knew I had to tell him what I'd been up to.

The following night on our walk I told him I had something to tell him. I was serious and he looked pretty worried. I'm not sure that is something any husband wants to hear from their wife.

I pulled the folded up yellow paper out of my pocket and handed it to him. As he read I waited for his reaction. I had no idea how he was going to react. I'd literally went behind his back to God. I'd made it clear that I didn't want him following my feelings or his. We would continue to pray for God's direction. To me it was becoming clear that God had given him everything he'd wanted in a job. In return he'd given up what God had called him to. Serving in the local church and serving with us.

    I had to realize that my prayers being answered was amazing. Prayer works. My Bible study was right. Fight the real enemy with the weapons God gave us to use. But we were behind on every bill. This didn't make any sense. This didn't look like faith. This looked irresponsible. That small voice was still saying, "This is all going to be ok." I didn't know how. If Bubba chose God, I knew God would honor that and take care of us. We trusted Him.

Hebrews 10:24-25 And let us consider how we may spur one another on toward love and good deeds, not giving up meeting together, as some are in the habit of doing, but encouraging one another- and all the more as you see the Day approaching.

Chapter 17

Bubba continued to pray and ask for confirmations. The more he prayed the more he knew exactly what he was going to do. He was going to choose God over this job. Now the only question was when. Should we wait until we were more financially stable? The next couple months would be really busy at his work. We definitely have the opportunity to get caught up on bills. Even save a bit until he found other work.

He knew what he needed to do. He was choosing God now. Not when it was more convenient. Not when we felt more secure. There was only one question we really needed to answer. Do we trust God now? Do we trust Him to come through now? He is not asking us to micromanage the situation a bit before we follow. He is asking us to trust Him and follow Him now.

On the following Monday Bubba went to his boss to put in his two week notice. As bubba walked out the door that morning. I cried, "Lord, you know what you're doing. Thank you for a husband brave enough to follow when it makes no sense at all. Lord, now we really need your help."

Bubba received a call the very next morning that this would be his last day. We were expecting this. We knew this meant even less money for the bills. Bill collectors could care less if God told you to quit or not.

Keep in mind the editors are still waiting to hear back from us. There was no way I could go to Bubba. The money wasn't there. I knew if God wanted me to do it He could come up with the money. I was comfortable with telling the publisher, "God can handle it. I'm waiting on him."

I still couldn't get out of my mind the few sentences I read of that sample edit. I'd only made it through the first paragraph before I had to stop. "That wasn't me," I thought. I knew in my head I was not capable of editing this manuscript myself. Everything online said you can't edit your own writing. If professional authors weren't allowed to edit their own stuff. How could I consider doing it?

Day after day we prayed for God's provision to pay our bills. To make matters worse the mortgage company was calling. If we didn't pay by the end of the week they were considering starting foreclosure papers the following Monday. Bubba was waiting on a check from a side job. We knew the check was enough to cover it. "God you've got this. Moving across the country was a lot scarier and you came through every time. I know you will do it again."

I needed to find truth. If I was scared I knew Bubba was even more scared. I kept remembering an example in a book I'd read when we were first saved. Bubba's coworker had given us a Duck Commander book. Lately, this one part kept coming up in my mind. I hadn't thought about that book in a long time until recently. The part I kept remembering was when Phil and Kay had just started their business and the bank note was due. The money wasn't there to pay it. Phil knew that God was in control.

God would provide. He went and checked the mail on the last possible day. A check came just in time to pay the bank note.

"God, I am standing on this truth. If you can do it in their lives you can do it in ours. We trust you just as much as they do." I ran to the shelf. Yes, I still had the book! I frantically flipped through the pages. I found the page and told Bubba it was all going to be ok. The check would come just like it did for Phil and Kay. As the mail lady came down the road that Friday morning. We waited expectantly.

Just like He always does. He provided. The check was there. We paid our mortgage. God would see us through whatever He was calling us to. We could trust Him.

Matthew 6:26-27 Look at the birds of the air; they do not sow or reap or store away in barns, and yet your heavenly Father feeds them. Are you not much more valuable than they? Can any one of you by worrying add a single hour to your life?

Chapter 18

On Monday I received a group email from Kitty Hawk Baptist Church. There was an emergency with one of the members. I immediately thought of all the older ladies we loved so much. What if something had happened to them? The email said nothing except an emergency and for us to pray. I texted the youth leader to get some details. She didn't have any information about the email. We decided to chat and catch up. I had a lot to tell her about Bubba quitting his job and about us having no idea how we would pay our bills. Telling her how faithful God had been with the check coming at just the right time. Also wanted to tell her and ask for prayers about editing. We had a great conversation. She laughed so much on that call as I nonchalantly described our crazy life circumstances. When I mentioned editing I think that was the first time I'd told her I'd written a book.

During our call she was interrupted and needed to call me back. Hopefully she was going to get information about that emergency email. A few minutes later my phone rang. I didn't think anything of it. After all I was waiting for her call. Though I could tell in her voice something was wrong. She asked if Bubba was home and if I could go to him and sit down. "Umm, no. Just tell me," I said. With strain in her voice she started the conversation that would change my life, "Pastor's been in a motorcycle accident. He's gone."

In that moment I didn't know what to believe or what to do. I wanted to yell at God. Everything anyone ever said about why people die went through my head. "His time wasn't up God! He wasn't done doing good for you! He still had work to do! Why were you done with Him? Even if you were. We weren't!"

I realized in those moments how selfish I can be. All I could think about was the book. What would Pastor have said about it? Actually, I knew what he would say. He was witty and I usually didn't get his jokes. But this time I'd planned to get it. After he'd read it I just knew he would comment on this one part. In chapter 4 I'd said, "I'll never know if he walked away from our many exchanges laughing to himself at my immaturity or irritated at my rudeness." Why had I written I'll never know? I knew I would know. I was prepared to walk up to him and he simply say, laughing or irritated. If I wasn't prepared I'd end up standing there like an idiot. I'd been preparing for when I saw him again. Now this side of heaven I'll never know.

I walked inside to tell Bubba. The words that spilled out of my mouth through tears were, "Pastor's gone and he'll never read my book." Had I been relying on his approval all along? I went into the kids' rooms to tell them. As the facts sunk in I realized I couldn't even call anyone. I was alone. I needed to reach out to people. I needed support.

The phone rings again. It's the publisher calling. I can't recall exactly what I said to Him. I'm sure through tears. I said something similar to, "Dude, you're the furthest thing from my mind. My pastor was killed today."

The world was coming down around us. Our only income was random side jobs, Pastors gone, and I'm supposed to be publishing a book. No way could we afford that. No way could we afford another trip back to the beach. All I wanted to do was walk into Kitty Hawk Baptist Church, sit on a pew, and hear the hymns I thought I disliked so much. I needed familiar things. I was too far away from everyone I needed. I needed my people. I reached out for prayer here but I needed the beach. I needed Kitty Hawk. I needed Mom's Group.

The following morning I received a package in the mail. This package was from the missionary from Bible study and VBS. The one that taught me what a missionary was. I had given the manuscript to four people. Hoping to get some feedback and advice. Well, she hadn't given me much feedback. I figured maybe she hadn't read it.

As I opened the package I found a book. Weird, but I trust her. She must have a reason. There wasn't an explanation. Just a note saying who it was from. I headed back to the porch where I'd been sitting all morning. Nothing on my mind except Pastor. One minute crying, one minute fine, and the next crying again. More people at the beach must've found out. My phone had been wringing non-stop all morning. Well-meaning people wanting to make sure we didn't find out through social media. Their hearts were in the right place. Although they didn't know I'd been living in my own little silent nightmare since a few hours after the accident. I was sitting on the porch to get away from the phone calls.

As I sat with the book on my lap I began to read. Within a few sentences I knew why God had her send me this book. It answered a question I didn't know I was seeking an answer to anymore. How would God provide the money to edit the book? He wouldn't. He didn't need to. Instead He provided the answer through this gift. Within a few sentences of reading this woman's testimony I realized her grammar wasn't perfect. She didn't sound fancy. And guess what? It didn't take from her story at all. If someone refuses to read my story because of my grammar. Than they weren't the one I wrote it for. I am not an author. I am simply a woman who is brave enough to follow God and do what He says. Even when it doesn't make any sense to anyone else. I would edit this book myself. He asked me to share our story. If He wanted someone else to write it. He would have asked them.

Although I was sure this was His direction I also knew I was very emotional about Pastor. I did not want to make any decisions based on feelings. I decided to wait a few days and pray about it.

That night as I lay in bed. Bubba already asleep next to me. My phone dings. "Probably another person making sure I know about Pastor," I think to myself. I check my phone. It's a text from the youth leader at the beach. She was offering to pay our way back to the beach for the funeral. I'd forgotten I'd even told her about our financial situation. As I fell asleep I knew in my heart God's got us all. He knows what is going on. He knows when we hurt. He knows what we need. Later I found out it wasn't just the youth leader who made our trip back possible. Others had gotten together to cover the costs.

I may not like it all the time. I may not understand it most of the time. But I will fall asleep tonight knowing tomorrow is another day. Another day I will follow the one who holds us all in His hands. Tomorrow may be hard. But I trust Him. He has proven again and again He is worth trusting.

Lamentations 3:22-23 Because of the LORD's *great love we are not consumed, for his compassions never fail. They are new every morning; great is your faithfulness.*

Chapter 19

The next morning I remembered a few weeks ago we became members at our new church in east Texas. In the letter containing the mission trip photo Pastor told us about some transfer letter Baptist churches do. He asked if when we took the step to join we'd let him know. I'd made sure the church knew they needed to send Pastor this letter. Did they send it in time? I asked our church if they'd sent it to him. I was relieved to hear they had. Now the only question was whether or not Pastor received the letter before the accident. I reached out to Kitty Hawk to see if Pastor ever found out we'd taken the step to join our new church. I'll never forget how I felt when I was told he'd received it. He'd written our transfer letter and it was mailed the morning of the accident.

Over the next week we waited for the letter to come. I couldn't help but feel like this was the last thing he'd ever say to us. How many times I'd never even cared what He thought. I blew off so many things he'd said to us. Especially in the months leading up to moving. We were in over our heads. We were stressed to the max. Relying on ourselves and taking it out on him. Now it felt like time was standing still as I waited to hear his last words to us.

While waiting for the letter I found a card in my purse. As I opened it I couldn't believe my eyes. It was from Pastor. About a month before leaving the beach we'd attended a birthday party for him. So consumed with the details of finding a house in Texas we hadn't gotten him a gift. On the way to the party we went by the grocery store. Grabbed eight small single serve pies and threw them in a bag. He loved pie. I remembered not even wanting to be there that day.

This card was a thank you note which I threw in my purse and never even opened. He'd written, "I know you're in an awkward time in between places right now, but be patient God will see you through." He knew all along we weren't really mad at him. We were just upset and struggling. The card was signed "Pastor & Jill". Everyone else called him Pastor Don, Pastor Teears, or simply Don. I always just called him Pastor.

A few days later the church notified us. The letter had come. We opened it and read his last words to us. It felt like for the first time I wanted to know what he had to say. So often I'd been annoyed by what he'd said to me. It seemed every time I interacted with him I felt like a kid with their parent. The Spirit was constantly pointing out things about my personality that needed to change. When I would sit in Sunday church and hear a message that convicted me it was him that delivered it. As the scripture says in Hebrews 12:11 No discipline seems pleasant at the time, but painful. Later on, however, it produces a harvest of righteousness and peace for those who have been trained by it.

The Holy Spirit used him on many occasions to deliver serious truths to me. Truths I needed to hear. Which I handled like a very immature Christian. Getting mad, pouting, but eventually changing. I knew whatever that letter said it would be exactly what we needed to hear. Even if it was correction. Remember towards the end we were not nice, holy Christians with humble hearts. We were stressed, angry, and relying on our own strength most of the time. Or at least that's how I remembered acting. As I began to read his letter. It wasn't what I expected at all. "The Henley family were active, vibrant, committed participants in our church until the time they relocated to TX. It is with regret that we had to say good-bye at their departure. It is with joy that we recommend them to you as faithful Christians and hard workers for the Body of Christ. You will be blessed by their involvement."

"Faithful Christians," I read in shock. Pastor wasn't fake at all. Never sugar coated anything for anyone. This means he actually saw us as 'faithful Christians'. Not as immature, rude kids trying to follow God. That's how I felt I'd treated him. 'Hard workers for the Body of Christ' not new Christians so on fire for Christ they often got in over their heads, take on too much, or organize events that fizzle out because it was their idea. No, he saw us as faithful Christians, hard workers, and thought our new church would be blessed by us. Meaning he'd not held a party when we left that beach. I was expecting that letter to say. "I will pray for you as you try to keep them in line. They have a long way to go. And Kelly she doesn't know how to think before she speaks." Praise God He wanted us to know how Pastor really saw us. Instead of how we saw ourselves.

Finally I had enough courage to call the publisher and tell them I was refusing their editing services. I was going to edit it myself. I knew what I needed to do. I was so emotional on the phone. I'm sure I sounded like a crazy person. At the end of the conversation he stated he'd leave the book in the editing queue.

Just in case I changed my mind. "If you need a plan 'b' that's great but I don't," thankfully I only thought that to myself.

After searching more online about how someone would edit their own writing. I found an article about editing it backwards. The article said it was the only way to take your own writing out of context. Ok. That's weird but may work. Looking online I realized that The Chicago Manual of Style is not a bunch of guys in Chicago that don't like my style. It's a book. I learned tighter writing is pretty easy to create. I also learned there is something seriously wrong with a comma splice. Best to just avoid those altogether.

I printed the latest manuscript. Deciding to edit it backwards on the way to the beach for Pastor's funeral. I began to have enough courage to tell family about the book. My insecurities seemed trivial at this point. I think a sudden death can have that effect on perspective. Pastor always spoke of a death pushing him towards ministry. Giving him a sense of urgency and seriousness. My fear seemed insignificant. Things were surely becoming more urgent. I may not have time to put off what God was asking me to do.

Esther 4:14 For if you remain silent at this time, relief and deliverance for the Jews will arise from another place, but you and your father's family will perish. And who knows but that you have come to your royal position for such a time as this?

Chapter 20

When we arrived back in east Texas Bubba reached out at church about a job. He was hired by a man we knew. He was looking for a full time worker and Bubba could fill the position.

We needed to give our full attention to the things God was calling us to. Right now we knew that was the book. Just praying we didn't lose the house in the process of following His direction. Knowing that if we did lose it. He would still be worth it. Realizing the amount of faith it took to say that and mean it only could have come from what we've walked through in the last two years. He will come through. We would trust Him to meet our needs.

The final manuscript was finished. Edited completely by me. Relying on the Spirit as much as I could. Having to daily rely on the confirmations He'd given us just to consider sending this thing back to them. I was terrified to send it back. I felt completely inadequate, unqualified, and foolish. Knowing I needed to do it afraid. I sent it back to them.

After receiving it they would send the revised manuscript back for me to approve for printing. Giving me one last chance to make any changes. When I received their email I accidently opened it into a different program. One I hadn't known was on the computer. This program had a "read aloud" option. As I sat and listened to the book it was so easy to see the mistakes I'd made. The quiet that was supposed to be quite. Little mistakes that I hadn't caught. I was able to catch sentences that just didn't make sense or that didn't sound like me. I sent it back to them after making all the changes I could find.

The day I received the final revised galley proof was one of the hardest days. They needed me to approve the manuscript for printing. Approving it meant I was either successfully accomplishing what God asked me to do or I was completely messing it up.

Knowing this was the no turning back point in the process was one of the scariest places I'd been. The doubts were so loud. The what if's were consuming me. As I tried to sleep that evening I was not finding any rest. My chest was hurting and my fears were consuming me. As I came out to the living room. I remembered a sermon on social media I'd wanted to watch earlier in the day. As I watched, my walls came tumbling down. I sobbed for probably an hour in my living room. I shared the sermon and wrote this post.

November 19, 2019- "Praise God for not being able to sleep. For the time to hear God's truth through this message. I felt crushed with the pressure of finishing the final stages. Often I only see the ways I'm capable of messing this up. My stronghold- I doubt often He could actually use me or would want to.

I know He doesn't make mistakes. I know He meant to choose me. Do I believe I'm actually capable? No, I don't. Do I believe He's capable? Without a doubt, yes! Do I sometimes feel He should have chosen someone else? Unfortunately, yes. Chosen someone who didn't spend the whole week stressing. Trying to make sure everything was just right. While not opening her own Bible once. Chosen someone who hasn't been at a breaking point all week. Yet, instead of surrendering she held strong. Chosen someone who isn't in the very strongholds she was years ago.

It's true God uses the weak. Does it mean I feel strong while being used? No. It's true God doesn't call the qualified. He qualifies the called. Does it mean I feel qualified? No.

I have enough faith to know I will obey. I won't give up. I will do this. I will tell our story. I will tell of His faithfulness. I will share my heart for the local church. I will share of His goodness. But being at a place where only God can come through, hurts.

The funny thing is, I feel better now. Yes, right now curled up. Worn out from a major, ugly crying session. This feeling is better than I've felt all week as little miss tough girl. A tough girl holding it all together. The plates I was balancing just came crashing down. But the truth is they were never mine to hold in the first place. He knows what I need to do. He wants to help me. Yet all week I snatched them from Him. While saying, 'You called me. So I can do it.'

No! He can do it. All He wants me to do is let go. To just let Him lead. I was never meant to carry this load. I was never meant to lead."

To my surprise the church whose sermon I'd shared commented on the post. "Beautiful words!!! Real and Raw!!! What great traits for God to work with!!! All He wants is us... the mess, the tears, the joy, the happiness...whatever we choose to bring! His goal is for us to lay it at His feet...that's where the Masterpiece begins!!! Head up. Eyes fixed...you have work to do!!! You are equipped with everything needed to move ahead... you are His!!!!"

The following day I sent the approval to the publisher. This was it. All I could think was, "God you better know what you're doing because I don't." Over the next few days I really tried to let it sink in. If this worked, if this book would actually change lives, it had nothing to do with me, and my abilities. It had everything to do with Him and what He wanted to accomplish. What He wanted to use us for.

The publisher contacted us on November 25, 2019 the manuscript had been cleared for printing. Eight months after beginning this journey it was finished. The lessons and struggles molded and strengthened our faith. He'd always see us through everything He called us to.

1 Timothy 2:3-4 This is good, and pleases God our Savior, who wants all people to be saved and to come to a knowledge of the truth.

Chapter 21

Recently Bubba has been serving, involved in ministry, and faithfully attending Bible studies. I'd sit and watch him at the dining room table in the evenings reading and studying the scriptures while preparing for Bible study. Many times I've watched him and thanked God for taking him away long enough to give him a new hunger for the Lord.

God is strengthening His faith. God has brought revival to his heart. In a few short weeks Bubba will be heading on his first mission trip without us. If we were still at the beach. If I still thought the way I used to. I would be upset that he was going without us. But I'm not that same person anymore. I couldn't be happier Bubba will be serving alongside other men from the church. In my opinion, the best part is God will be able to show him how strong his faith really is. How capable he is as the spiritual leader of this home. How called he is to lead us.

It's probably been hard for him to feel like the spiritual leader with me in his way. In the beginning I attended about five Bible studies a week. I gained the knowledge quickly. I'm also very vocal and involved with many ministries. Bubba took it at a much slower pace. Probably because of me being such a fanatic new Christian. I'm glad God is getting me out of the way.

The mission team would be gone on Valentine's Day. I began to have ideas about the kids and I hosting a Valentine's Day fellowship at the house. I knew I needed to pray about this. I know my personality and I know my weaknesses. Was I just trying to keep myself busy while he was gone? Was God actually calling me to do this? I spent the next few weeks praying and asking God to confirm if this was what I should do. I knew why I wanted to do it. I knew it seemed like a good idea. The fellowship would be for any women that may be spending Valentine's Day alone. I now knew what it felt like to be alone. With the church in our lives none of us have to be alone. But was this God's idea or mine. Not all good ideas are God's ideas. I didn't want to be involved in anything God hadn't planned for me to do. If I continued praying He'd confirm if I should do this.

I'd learned this lesson recently with the need for a homeschool group in the area. Not having a homeschool group was one of the hardest things about living here. I knew there were homeschoolers here. I felt they just didn't know each other.

When we were searching for a church. We met at least one or two homeschool families at each church. Most families telling us the same thing, "There aren't very many homeschoolers around here." Well, clearly there were. They just didn't know each other. As month after month went on I really felt I would be involved in starting a group. Yet He wasn't giving me the go ahead. Often I would pray, "God, it wasn't an accident I met all those homeschoolers. Or that you keep bringing their statements to my mind."

The timing just wasn't right. I really felt the main snag in the group would be where to meet. Our church didn't have a playground. Which I felt was a necessity with smaller children. I really felt the main thing this area missed was fellowship. Just plain old socializing for the moms and the kids. As I sat here in this small town for almost a year without a group I didn't miss the organized classes and field trips. I missed the moms I shared life with. I missed my kids having like-minded friends.

I knew we had the option to meet at a park. Yet He wasn't giving me the ok. Many times I wanted to just pick a day, a time, and post on a local social media page. He wasn't agreeing. Something in my spirit kept reminding me. "What are you going to do when people are expecting to meet and because of weather you can't?" I knew without a doubt a park wouldn't be right. The group needed consistency. A consistent place for moms and kids to be together. I would wait. I would wait for His best.

Finally the day came when another local homeschool mom came to me about starting a group together. She'd just started attending a church that used to be the homeschool group in the area. The pastor and his wife were former homeschool parents. Their kids had since graduated and the group hadn't met in a while. Though they would love nothing more than to be the place for a new group in the area.

Still taking a week or two to pray. Because I wanted this group to bare the fruit of fellowship, support, and changed lives. I wanted God's best. This seemed great but was it His best. I wanted to be sure. As He continued to press on my heart this group and this church. I knew this was it. After waiting over a year God came through. Like He always does. This church not only had a pastor with a heart for homeschooling. This church also had a covered, fenced playground. A gym, class rooms, and a fellowship hall. In addition it had a youth room complete with pool table, foosball, and air hockey.

Each week our group faithfully has around twenty kids. I know without a doubt this group was planned and prepared by God. He'd went ahead of us and prepared this for us. We just needed to trust His timing. Trust He had it all figured out. He would've let me meet at that park. Though I wouldn't have experienced His best as I do now each week. I didn't accomplish this. I simply waited for His perfect timing. I watch the kids run from the vehicles to their new friends. I thank God He allowed me to be part of His plan. As I hear the kids saying they count down the days until group. I thank God I waited until we could meet at a consistent place. Most of all I thank God for one more situation that strengthened my faith. Reassuring me He will come through. He will do what He's promised. If He's called me to something He will see me through it. If I wait on Him I can have His best.

Ecclesiastes 3:1 There is a time for everything, and a season for every activity under the heavens.

Chapter 22

As we continue on this path God has laid out for us we are amazed. Amazed at His faithfulness to prepare us in advance for events we don't even know are coming. Each and every time God comes through I can't help but question why others wouldn't want to live like this. Why others wouldn't want to know that someone bigger than them knows what is going on? To have someone who can literally see into your future and know what is ahead. And cares about you enough to prepare you for it.

Sometimes, I criticize the example I'm setting to non-believers. I question whether I should be so open about our struggles. I think often, "Am I going to cause people to think being a Christian is bad?" I pray you don't think that. Majority of my struggles are because of my pride, independence, and stubbornness. I try so hard to do what is right. Yet, I fight surrendering. I struggle to hold it all together. I act like I have enough experience now and fall on my face. I see other Christians who face way scarier things than me and they don't handle it like a crazy person. God is still working on me. I'm doing my best to grow, change, and surrender more. But this is real. This is the real stuff I've went through and am going through. I won't pretend it isn't happening. You deserve to know sometimes change is hard. Sometimes it takes making the same mistake over and over until you realize things need to be done differently.

God is worth it. That is why I continue working through my mess. He is completing in me the work He began. Each time the fight is shorter. Each time my pride takes a backseat a little quicker.

I get upset with others because they're missing freedom. The freedom that comes with surrender. When we choose to think we are ultimately the boss we never get His best. We are always settling for the version of reality we can create. Never His best. Simply our best. When in comparison our best is rags. I can become so angry because I want people to experience what our family has experienced. The fulfilling, life giving freedom that comes only from surrendering our will to His.

I could've made that post about meeting at the park. Having a family or two show up occasionally when the weather was permitting. But I waited. I waited for Him. His timing was perfect and His plan for the group was perfect. Now the group is not only bearing fruit in our lives but in the lives of other families. When we surrender our will to His we're not the only ones who'll be affected and blessed by our obedience. We have the opportunity to experience a freedom matched by nothing else this world has to offer and be a blessing to others.

In the weeks following the book release I learned I still have a lot to learn. His work in me is not finished. I know that I will continue to seek Him. I will continue to choose Him. I will continue to strive to pray and wait on Him. In reality it seems that the world's views are creeping in around every corner. As soon as I take my eyes off of Him the enemy swoops in with his schemes and reasoning. In that moment I stare too long at my responsibility to God's call. I begin to obsess about all the things I should be doing to accomplish what God has called me to.

Pertaining to the book I became obsessed with how to make it as successful as I could. How to be a good steward of the opportunity God gave me. I began to look at how others were achieving success. After all I didn't know what I was doing. All while forgetting God knows what He is doing.

I've realized my biggest stumbling block is my imagination. I justify my planning and imagining by saying it's for His glory. Just trying to be the best me I can be. When in reality He is using me as I am. Not as I wish I could be.

He didn't ask someone to write a book who was great at self-promotion. He didn't ask someone who was confident with the new title of author. He asked me. The girl with no idea what she is doing or why He'd choose her. The girl just wanting people to find the same freedom she did. The girl who just wants people to go to church. Wants people to stop making up lies like, "Jesus isn't just at church. That's why I don't go." To be clear no one ever said Jesus was only at church. People tell you to go to church because church is where you learn how to walk with Jesus. Where you learn how to change things in your life. Because you need to change. You can't carry around your old self while wanting a new life. Your new identity in Christ needs to come with accepting the old is no longer a part of you. That means with His help you can let go of the baggage that is keeping you from His best in your life.

I'm learning success isn't measured the same way in God's eyes as it's measured in the world. *We Will Follow* doesn't need to be on the best sellers list to be successful. It doesn't even need to sell a hundred copies. This book may never help us be more financially stable and that's ok. If this book changes just one life than it was worth every sleepless night, tear, and insecurity I had to get over. If this book helps one person realize they're chosen and loved by their Creator than it was all worth it. That's success. That is why we do what we do. Because people's lives may be changed. We may reach one person who then reaches another and another. Growing the church one person at a time.

Acts 16:5 So the churches were strengthened in the faith and grew daily in numbers.

Chapter 23

Sometimes it takes time to know if we've made the right choices. We just hold onto the promises and confirmations. We just know we listened, followed the best we could, and then wait on Him.

As the book made it into more and more hands the feedback started coming in. I was beginning to hear a lot about how much the book sounded like me. Comments saying they felt like they were having a conversation with me. "Thank you Lord for giving me the ability and courage to edit the book myself."

Other comments referring to the importance of the church. Christians being encouraged in their roles in the local church. "Lord they are getting it! They are seeing the point! Seeing my heart for the local church. Thank you for allowing me to do this." This book wasn't just our story. It was His story all along. Our lives were not ours anymore. We'd found what we were made for and that was to proclaim His story of redemption in our lives.

Throughout this writing process I knew I'd write more. I couldn't explain why I knew I just did. At first I wasn't happy about that feeling. I'd hoped one book would be enough. I would write *We Will Follow* and then spend forever trying to get people to read it. Although that didn't feel like the reality I would be living. He began to change my heart and I began to look forward to writing more. If He was going to use our story to reach people through books than we were all in.

I really felt led to write a devotional. A devotional for adult, unchurched new believers. That may seem very specific. Yet I think there are a lot of us. I was twenty seven years old when I first arrived on the church scene. I had no background with churchy words and Bible stories. As I'd attend Bible studies and start spending time around Christians I began to realize they all knew a lot that I didn't. Bible stories would be mentioned and everyone, but me, knew what had been referred to. "Faith like Noah," I had no idea what Noah had done. "Courage like Daniel," I had no idea who Daniel was. Or hearing words and phrases like, "The Word became flesh." I felt I'd entered into a world where everyone spoke the same language except me. I received a devotional at the time, meant to bless me, and help me on my new walk. Yet it did nothing more than make me feel even less capable of figuring this all out. The person's heart was in the right place. I just didn't have the background they had.

I'd been working on the plans for this devotional off and on while completing the publishing process of *We Will Follow*. Planning to have a 365 day devotional. Complete with a churchy words dictionary in the back. This was going to be so great. Once the publishing process ended, and the initial release was slowing down, I was confident it was time to really start working on the devotional.

Week after week very little progress was being made with the devotional. At one point in the process of publishing *We Will Follow* I'd started a second book. Picking up right where we'd left off. Though I never made it past the fifth chapter. I had moved onto the devotional I was so excited about. Still, week after week something wasn't right. This wasn't working.

As I began to pray and seek His direction. Because I knew full well I couldn't do this without Him. Nor did I want to. He began to press on me about the other book I'd started. "No Lord. That's not the plan. I'm doing the devotional now. I've already told people about it. They are excited. Just let me do that one first."

After another week of praying I gave in. I decided to spend time reading through both the beginning of the second book and the devotional. Hoping He'd give me direction on which one He wanted me to do first. I began to read the second book. I barely made it through the first couple chapters before I was crying. Realizing why I wanted to do the devotional first.

It hadn't been an urgent desire to get the devotional into the right hands. I simply didn't want to face the hurt in the second book. The pain I'd feel from reliving Bubba working out of town. Or the pain that would come with writing about Pastor. I knew I needed to write *We Will Trust*. The devotional would come when the time was right. He knows what He's doing. He knows there is someone that needs to hear what is on the pages of this book. And for them it was worth writing it.

Psalm 31:14 But I trust in you, LORD; *I say, "You are my God."*

Chapter 24

In *We Will Follow* I chose not to include a prayer of salvation. For what I thought was a good reason. Yet, I'm learning it's not my place to micromanage Jesus. I didn't want someone saying a prayer. Accepting Jesus into their heart. While sitting in their home and never stepping foot into a church. Never learning how to walk with God. Never learning how to walk out their new self. When someone accepts Jesus they are a new creation. I feared if they've only known their old self. How would they learn to walk in newness of life? They would just continue living in bondage.

Heaven should simply be the bonus of an amazing life here. I'm not saying that nothing bad happens when you are walking with Jesus. What I'm saying is you don't have to walk alone.

You have a loving Father who wants only the best for you. Regardless of how your earthly father was. Your heavenly Father is perfect. He chose you and created you. The world we live in is bad. Yet, the bad doesn't have to consume us. We live in this world but our minds are not consumed by it.

Life isn't just making it work in a messed up world. We are not meant to just survive. We are meant to thrive. Our lives may not look successful in the world's eyes. We may not have all the earthly treasures such as money, fame, status, and possessions. I may never have those things. That's ok because you know what I do have. I have a new family tree. I have two Jesus believing kids with servant's hearts. I have been a first-hand witness to someone who had been in bondage to drugs, alcohol, guilt, and shame for years be set free. To hear peace in the voice of a person who you've heard so much torment for so many years is a feeling I would never trade for all the riches this world has to offer. To know the tears shed and prayers that went up for this person were heard. To ultimately know them witnessing my faith walked out may have played a part in them surrendering it all to their creator. If God used my walk to help Him reach them. I'm in. I'm all in. This world can have all its riches. I don't want it. I want to see lives changed. I want to be available for the next time He wants to use me.

In this book I'm choosing not to micromanage Jesus. I'm including a prayer to help you if you have decided you're ready for a new life. Are you sick and tired of the same junk over and over and you want to live the life that was planned for you?

God is real. He really has plans for you and they are good plans. He really loved us so much that He sent His only son, Jesus, to die for us on a cross. He died to pay the price for what we've done. He died for all people. Not just a certain few. All. You are definitely included. After three days Jesus really conquered death and rose from the grave. Jesus really said that He's the only way to the Father. If anyone has ever told you there is another way they are lying and do not know The Way. Do you trust them enough to not only bet eternity on it but to bet your life while here on earth?

I'm not telling you to blindly accept what I'm saying. That's not what I did. I dug and researched through different translations and denominations. With no church background at all He was still able to direct me. I promise He can direct you too. He was not threatened by my questions or my searching. He is not threatened by yours either. We have a big God. He is big enough to handle our questions.

If you decided today to follow Jesus I beg you to seek out a church. Do not become a new creation while trapped in your old self. If someone tells you that you can be a Christian and not go to church. They are right. You can put a Christian label on yourself. While living in complete bondage to the same junk you wanted to see change on the day you decided to follow Jesus. If you want a new life and truly live like a new creation than you need to do things differently.

Don't be afraid of the things you may need to change. If you are honestly and earnestly seeking Him He will change your heart. Some changes will hurt. Usually these are the ones we've held onto the longest. Things we've found our identity in. He wants to give you a new identity but in order to experience it you have to let go of the old identity. Just like anything else He may ask you to do. He's promised to help you through it. He will help you change the things about you that need to change. Seek Him with all your heart. Seek Him like your life depends on it. Sometimes I think I had a lot of junk to overcome so I had to fight a little harder than others. That's ok.

If you've decided to follow Jesus or have simply realized you've been living a lie. Maybe, you've been living with a Christian label while still holding onto your old self. Maybe you should say this prayer too. I've heard revival feels the same as being born again.

Maybe today is the day you become a new creation. Maybe today is the day you allow revival in your heart. Either way you need Jesus to accomplish this. This prayer is not the end. It is only the beginning of this journey with Jesus. This may be your first day hearing about another way or you may have been in church most of your life. Either way the angels are rejoicing. Because today you gave your all for the one that gave His all for you.

Lord, I need you. I can't change me. Only your power working through me can. Take everything in my heart that will stand up against you. I know I've sinned. Please forgive me. I need you to save me. I know you chose me. Help me to learn more about you. Help me to seek you above all else. Bring others around me to help me seek you and to learn more about you. Thank you for sending Jesus for me. Help me to remember all you have done for me. Each and every day help me remember you. Amen.

Did you pray that prayer? If so than this is the first day of the rest of your life. Take this seriously! This is huge! Find yourself a church that follows Jesus. Remember He is the only way. Allow Him to change your heart. Don't forget you're not an innocent bystander in this. You need to actively participate in this. God is not a genie. So don't treat Him like one. He is not here to grant your wishes. He is here to make you a new creation through Jesus. This takes getting rid of the old. Only by using His strength will this be possible. Surrender the plans for your life to Him. Let Him lead. Trust that He wants what's best for you. He has a plan for you. Seek Him, learn, and grow. You will make mistakes. Choose to learn from them. Don't condemn yourself. You are learning. You are growing. He will be there to help you. He can be trusted.

2 Corinthians 5:17 Therefore, if anyone is in Christ, the new creation has come. The old has gone, the new is here!

Chapter 25

Finding a local church is one of the most important things you need to do. You need support. You need guidance. You need to learn how to put on your new self. Don't expect the people in the church to be perfect. I promise they're not. They are just broken people. Trying to put on and walk out their new selves just like you. When they let you down. Forgive them. Take it to the Father. Meaning talk to God about it and pray for them. Do not run around talking to everyone else about it. And most importantly stay put. Do not leave the church God calls you to because of people failing you. Only when God calls you out will you leave your church home. Otherwise you will leave that next church as soon as something doesn't go your way. You'll become like a homeless church person. Seek His guidance, find your church home, and grow. There will be peace when God calls you from the church He sent you to. You will not leave offended!

In the church some people may get on your last nerve often. Grow! You need to grow. You need to learn how to handle people better. You may go to a church that plays music you don't like. Grow! Learn that church is not about being entertained. You may go to a church with way too many people not helping out.

You are serving to the max, and getting burnt out. Grow! Learn how to say no. Learn how to seek His guidance on what areas you are being called to serve in. Learn to encourage others to serve. Sometimes people can hear a need and not think they are qualified. Yet, if you walked up to them and asked, "Hey would you like to help with the clothes drive?" Who knows maybe they've been praying someone would ask them.

My point is don't change churches because things aren't the way you like. If God called you there. Than you are to be a part of the solution not the problem. Who knows, maybe the whole reason He sent you there was to make you get over yourself? Helping you to seek Him above your preferences.

I think that's why He sent me to Kitty Hawk Baptist Church. I needed to get over myself. I was very self-centered. Wanted the music my way, the lights my way, some of the people drove me nuts, and Pastor got on my nerves. I wanted things to be different. Wanted more families. Yet, I knew He called me there. The more I wanted to go to another church but instead I stayed, the more I grew. The more I learned to look to Him. I learned that the church sermons were not meant to entertain me. They were meant to convict and change me. I learned how to see the music as worship to God not entertainment for me. I learned how to handle people better. How to forgive them as Christ had forgiven me. I grew to love everything about Kitty Hawk even the things I didn't like.

The funny thing is the stuff I disliked became the things I long for now. Sitting here in east Texas at my new church with the lights, the music, and the families. On those rare occasions when an old hymn starts I'm almost brought to my knees. Those are the songs of my foundation. Those songs make me remember where I came from and the God I serve. They remind me of a Pastor who never got with the times of just telling people what they wanted to hear. Thank God, because I needed convicted. I needed to hear how God really wanted me to behave. I needed to change! I needed to grow! So do you! It won't be easy but it's worth every ounce of pride you get rid of and every tear you shed. God will help you and will be with you. He knows what you need. Trust Him with the church He sent you to. Make roots, trust the people, and most of all trust Him with your path.

I pray your journey has just begun. Be excited the best is yet to come. He is worth it. He can be trusted. You are chosen. You are loved. There is a plan for your life and it's a great one.

Ephesians 4:1-3 As a prisoner for the Lord, then, I urge you to live a life worthy of the calling you have received. Be completely humble and gentle; be patient, bearing with one another in love. Make every effort to keep the unity of the Spirit through the bond of peace.

Chapter 26

Each day that passes I grow more. Each Bible study I attend I gain new knowledge. Knowledge that I choose to use to change my life. Each obstacle we face I trust God more. Every believer has the same opportunity. That includes you.

I heard recently in Bible study someone refer to the homework as heart work. It's probably a normal churchy term people don't think much of. Yet those words are so accurate. When attending a Bible study you literally have the chance to experience a heart change. It may be hard. Ok, it will probably be hard. But it's so worth it. Recently we've been doing a study about our thought closets. I hadn't really given any thought to my thoughts. Go figure! Other than I have a lot of them. Majority of the time my thoughts and imagination control me. I used to think, "Well at least I trusted God eventually and let him lead."

Through this study I was learning it wasn't ok to just let my thoughts and feelings control me. I made it a point to do some honest heart work each morning with the book. As I did the Spirit showed me how unorganized my thought closet was. I had so much going on in my head. I wasn't able to focus on Him. What He was prompting me to do was get a planner. Weird. After a few days of praying about it. I decided, "Whatever you say God." I got the planner.

I've learned the Holy Spirit's little nudges don't have to make sense to me. When you literally have someone peering into your past, present, and future. Seeing what is tripping you up at that very moment. It's pretty cool. Actually it's amazing. I didn't need to know why. I just needed to get it. So I did. I searched for a Christian planner. I found one with places for prayers, daily reminders, and scriptures. I began writing down my schedule, prayers, songs I liked, and my to-do lists. So strange for me. I haven't had a planner since high school. Within days I felt like a new person. I was focusing better. I was less stressed. I really didn't have much stuff going on. It was just so jumbled in my head.

With my thoughts organized it was easier to focus on the Spirit. Allowing Him to get my attention concerning the next heart change I needed to face. The Spirit informed me I wasn't really trusting Him. To others it probably looked like I was. But really I'd practically have a panic attack, exhaust all my efforts, give up, and then let Him lead. That's not trusting Him. That's using God as my back up plan.

I'm also not trusting Him by refusing to admit He'd choose me to write books. By refusing to admit that I'm a Christian author. I'm saying God made a mistake when He chose me to do this. That is not trust.

I want to grow. I want to change. I'll listen and learn from my mistakes. I'm taking this one just as serious as the rest. Because the Spirit is right. I'm not trusting. I know the best time to have a breakthrough is when the Spirit is pointing it out. As I learned in the last study I needed to fight this tendency in me with the Word of God. I needed to use weapons that worked. The ones He'd given me to use.

2 Timothy 1:7 For the Spirit God gave us does not make us

timid but gives power, love and self-discipline. I'd read this scripture many times. I needed to dig deeper into it. In order to understand it better. Let's start at the beginning. "For the Spirit God gave us." Meaning it isn't something I'm still working to get. I have it. Yet, I'm not walking out the rest of this verse. Ok, I have the Spirit and His Spirit doesn't make me timid. As I looked up the word 'timid'. I was blown away. Timid doesn't mean quiet. Which is what I thought. Timid means showing a lack of courage or confidence, easily frightened. Wow! This whole time when God asked me to step out in faith I proceeded to flip out, panic, pout, whine, and exhaust all my efforts. All out of a lack of confidence and fear. "If that wasn't the spirit God gave me what spirit was I giving into?" Yep, you guessed it. There's an enemy and he is real tricky.

Let's keep digging into this scripture. "But gives us power," I also looked this word up. Figuring the way we use the word power is not what He meant. I was correct. Power means the ability to do something or act in a particular way. Interesting! So now I know I shouldn't be lacking confidence. I shouldn't be afraid. Because I have the power through the Spirit God gave me to act a different way. Oh, I was mad, "The enemy had been playing me all along!"

Continuing on to "Love." I decided to look it up. "Which Love is used in 2 Timothy 1:7?" In this verse the Love used is Agape Love. Oh, now that stopped me in my tracks. I've heard a lot about that love. That's not my love. That's not the kind of love I have for my husband, kids, or friends. This kind of love is God's love. This would definitely explain why I struggle with loving some people. Why I never understood why this verse didn't feel true of me. I knew I had the Spirit. Yet, some people I didn't even want to talk to let alone love them. Because of the Spirit God gave me I have the ability to love those people. These people that I struggle loving deserve for me to use the Spirit's power in me to love them. My effort or feelings were never going to be enough. I needed to rely on what the Spirit already gave me. Last part, self-discipline. The ability to control ones feelings and overcome ones weaknesses, the ability to pursue what one thinks is right despite temptations to abandon it. I have the ability to choose what's right because of Him.

Each time God prompts me to step out of my comfort zone I need to ask myself, "Who will I follow?" As I'm learning to walk this out I've had many opportunities to practice.

I'm learning to recognize though I may feel afraid or nervous. It's in that moment I need to seek God. In that moment I need to call out to Him for courage to walk out what He's asking me to do. Not after I've panicked, planned, and exhausted all my efforts.

Looking back on our story I see how deceived I was. I'm determined not to fall for the same schemes of the enemy again. How long I'd believed it was a normal part of a Christian life to be terrified and lack confidence. I thought it was normal to bounce off closed doors like a ping pong ball. Y'all it doesn't have to be that way. I could've prayed, trusted, and waited for His direction.

I'd look at other Christians and think, "One day I'll have faith like them." Truth was, I had the same faith as them. I just didn't know how to walk it out. I didn't know when I received the Holy Spirit I also received the ability to not be feelings driven. To not be consumed by my emotions. Even if that's my first reaction. I don't have to let it control me. The new creation I'd become was still being covered up by the old self I was carrying around. I want you to know this scripture is true for you too. 2 Timothy 1:7 For the Spirit God gave us does not make us timid, but gives us power, love, and self-discipline.

It may take practice to change our patterns of thinking. You have the ability given to you by the Spirit God gave you. Walk it out. Quit falling for the enemies schemes. He wants to trip you up and keep you in bondage. Use the weapons God gave you.

I've also come to accept death is unavoidable. 100% of the people I know, myself included, will die one day. I finally understand what having hope in eternity means. For those that have a personal relationship with Jesus death on earth is not the end. It's just the beginning of spending eternity with Jesus. Where they'll be joined by all the others with a relationship with Him. Realizing that everyone I know or will ever meet will die is not shocking. What's shocking is the fact not all of them will be meeting me in heaven. The fact I'm still here means I have time to reach more people. He's giving me the opportunity to be a part of His plan to reach His people. The people He placed before me on my path, like Pastor, didn't take for granted the days they were permitted to reach the lost. I don't want to waste any more time being scared of the calling placed on my life. Or the responsibility I have to those He places along my path. My hope is for everyone to be in heaven when they leave this place. Even more I want them to realize the significance of the fact they're still here now. To understand the responsibility they have to those around them.

2 Corinthians 10:4-5 The weapons we fight with are not the weapons of the world. On the contrary, they have divine power to demolish strongholds. We demolish arguments and every pretension that sets itself up against the knowledge of God, and we take captive every thought to make it obedient to Christ.

Donald Brian Teears "Pastor"
May 5, 1958- September 23, 2019

I'll always remember Pastor's heart for reaching bikers. If you'd like to help continue his passion please use this website LONDONBRIDGE.ORG. To reach the local chapter of F.A.I.T.H RIDERS he worked closely with.

Pastor's true story of faith
How One Boy Died So that I Might Live

KELLY R. HENLEY

HOW ONE BOY DIED SO THAT I MIGHT LIVE

A True Story about My Life

BY DONALD BRIAN TEEARS

I was ten years old and had just started the most transforming week of my life at a summer camp. The Christian boys camp was nestled on a point along a water way. The goal of this facility was to have fun teaching boys about the lessons of life from the Bible. No one could have known, when the week began, that amidst the cabins, canoes and campfires a tragedy so deadly would bring me life. One boy died so that I would live.

This camp, like hundreds of others, had bare-bulb rustic cabins with patched screen windows and a door that creaked when it opened. The bunk beds had well-worn, lumpy mattresses, which were occasionally put on the roof to dry. I got a top bunk. At night, the bathhouse was located with a flashlight, as you stepped gingerly over small sharp stones and pine needles. And the counselors tried to quiet down giggles and animal noises inside the cabin after all was dark. But on this night, like the night before, soft sobbing could be heard. The counselor asked me if everything was alright. How could it be? We had all been shocked and were living under a dark cloud, even though the days were warm and bright. Camp was supposed to be fun. I was not having fun. I was having something much more important, a crisis of the soul. For the first time in my life I realized how fragile my life was, and, how quickly if could end. That's because I watched a boy my age die.

My week at camp began the way it was supposed to, with early morning bugle revelry, racing over dew covered fields for singing, marching, games and crafts. Even meal times in the Mess Hall were part of the excitement that a good Christian camp utilized to draw kids into God's created world for our lessons on life. At archery we learned to aim for God's will in our life. At horseback riding we learned that when God controls our life we are more productive. At sailing we learned God's power like the wind is unseen but can be trusted. Of course, the Chapel times presented Jesus Christ as the Savior and source of eternal life.

Nothing had provoked my cabin's excitement more than our scheduled time at the Rifle Range. Most of us would be shooting a .22 caliber rifle for the first time. The prospect of this activity made me feel older, more mature and trusted. I couldn't wait. My cabin was scheduled for Wednesday afternoon.

At the appointed hour we all raced to the Rifle Range. We arrived a little early and watched another cabin of boys finishing up their session. Our counselor carefully instructed us to remain seated on the benches behind the firing line. Some of the other boys were still shooting.

Everyone was talking, some bragging, others asking questions. I guess that's how one of the boys on the firing line got distracted. He only shot 4 of the 5 rounds he had loaded into his rifle. Nobody knew the gun still had live ammo. The Range Instructor signaled for all the guns to be put down. They were. And then, the boys who had just shot were released to retrieve their targets. As everyone was checking their scores, one of the boys from my cabin left the bench, picked up the gun that was loaded, aimed down the range and squeezed the trigger. You can never get a bullet back. It was innocent and unintentional. It was an accident, but it was fatal.

Time slowed down for me. What I saw was unforgettable and dreamy. After all these years the boy from another cabin still falls the same way, struck in the head with a .22 caliber bullet. I can hear the desperate voice of the counselor who cradled the wounded and dying boy in his arms. He screams for someone to run for help. I ran up the sandy path that led to the nearest building where adults would be- the Craft Shop.

They couldn't believe me. It was unthinkable. Soon, more boys arrived at the Shop and a pickup truck was sent roaring down the path. It returned a short time later heading for the hospital. The police came and we were questioned. The little boy who was shot died two weeks later. Now, God was going to use his death to bring me life.

It's late Thursday night. The cabin counselor is trying to explain God's purpose in all this sadness. All I can think of is the dread of dying. If this boy died, I could die any moment. I'd heard the Gospel many times at home, at Church, at Camp, but now, I knew this message was for me. I figured Heaven was God's home, and He gets to decide who lives in it. Jesus was God's Son, so, if I was with Jesus I knew I'd get in too. I thought of Jesus like a ticket, my ticket into Heaven. Through my sobbing heart I asked God to save me, to give me Jesus, to please let me into His home forever. I know that's not very theological, but I was ten years old. God heard the prayer of my heart and saved me. I have never feared death again. I know that when I die I will be with Jesus. That's His promise.

I wonder how many other deaths God has used to bring life? The boy who died, I was told, was a Christian. I look forward to some day meeting him in Heaven and explaining God's way of using his death to give me life- eternal life. Many years later, after I had become a Pastor, I met the family of this boy and shared with them this turning point in my life. We cried tears for the sorrow of a life lost and tears of joy for my eternal life gained.

What you need to know to have eternal life.

1. You have said, done or thought something that is sinful and disqualifies you from being perfectly holy and living with God forever.

   "All have sinned and come short of the glory of God"~ Romans 3:23

2. God's penalty for just one sin is death.

   "The wages of sin is death."~ Romans 6:23

3. Jesus died on the cross to pay the penalty for your sin, because He loves you.

> *"God showed His love for us in that while we were yet sinners Christ died for us." ~ Romans 5:8*

4. Jesus offers you eternal life, if you will trust only in Him to save you.

> *"If you will believe in your heart, and confess with your mouth the Lord Jesus Christ, that God has raised Him from the dead, you shall be saved." ~ Romans 10:9*

5. Eternal life, forgiveness of sins and Heaven are gifts of God's grace. Ask Him to save you.

> *"Whosoever calls upon the name of the Lord shall be saved." ~ Romans 10:13*

Pastor's favorite verse
Galatians 2:20 I have been crucified with Christ; it is no longer I who live, but Christ lives in me; and the *life* which I now live in the flesh I live by faith in the Son of God, who loved me and gave Himself for me. NKJV

Pastor's favorite hymn
Be Thou My Vision (Slane)
Verse 1: Be thou my vision
    O Lord of my heart
    Naught be all else to me
    Save that Thou art
    Thou my best thought
    By day or by night
    Waking or sleeping

Thy presence my light

Verse 2: Be Thou my wisdom
 Be Thou my true Word
 I ever with Thee
 And thou with me Lord
 Thou my great Father
 I thy true son
 Thou in me dwelling
 And I with Thee one

Verse 3: Riches I heed not
 Nor man's empty praise
 Thou mine inheritance
 Now and always
 Thou and Thou only
 Be first in my heart
 High King of heaven
 My treasure Thou art

Verse 4: High King of heaven
 When vict'ry is won
 May I reach heaven's joys
 O bright heaven's Sun
 Heart of my own heart
 Whatever befall
 Still be my vision
 O Ruler of all

Colossians 2:12 Having been buried with him in baptism, in which you were also raised with him through your faith in the working of God, who raised him from the dead.

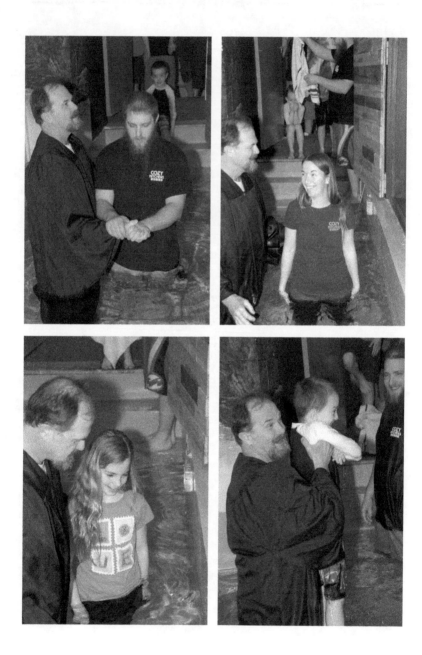

CPSIA information can be obtained
at www.ICGtesting.com
Printed in the USA
FSHW010043251120